LEGAL STUDIES SERIES

ARTHUR R. MILLER & HELEN HERSHKOFF

Class Action and New Forms of Aggregate Litigation in the United States

(BOCCONI CONFERENCE REPORTS MAY 10, 2024)

Foreword by
Marta Cartabia & Cesare Cavallini

BOCCONI UNIVERSITY PRESS

Copertina: Cristina Bernasconi, Milano
Impaginazione: Corpo4 Team, Milano

Copyright © 2024 EGEA S.p.A.
Via Salasco, 5 – 20136 Milano
Tel. 02/5836.5751 – Fax 02/5836.5753
egea.edizioni@unibocconi.it – www.egeaeditore.it

First edition: December 2024

ISBN (volume) 979-12-8162-760-4
ISBN (ebook) 979-12-8162-762-8

Stampa: Logo s.r.l., Borgoricco (PD)

TABLE OF CONTENTS

FOREWORD

By *Marta Cartabia** and *Cesare Cavallini***

If one topic underscores the close relationship between civil justice, its methods of implementation, and the fundamental rights enshrined in constitutions worldwide, it is undoubtedly access to justice. This is why the conference organized by the Department of Legal Studies at Bocconi University[1], which serves as the focus of this debut volume

---

* Professor Marta Cartabia is a Full Professor of Italian and European Constitutional Law at Bocconi University. Professor Cartabia is also President Emeritus of the Italian Constitutional Court, where she sat as a judge from 2011 to 2020. From 2021 to 2022, she served as Minister of Justice for Italian Prime Minister Mario Draghi. In 2009, she was a Straus Fellow at New York University School of Law, where she returned in 2023 to give the Keynote Address for the Class of 2023's Convocation. She served as Co-President to the International Society of Public Law (2021-2024) and she sits on the scientific and editorial boards of a number of academic law journals. In particular, she is currently member of the Advisory Board of the International Journal of Constitutional Law, co-editor-in-chief Quaderni Costituzionali, and co-editor-in-chief of the Italian Journal of Public Law. She currently serves as vice-President of the Commission for Democracy through Law of the Council of Europe (Venice Commission) where she sits since 2017.

** Professor Cesare Cavallini is a Full Professor of Civil Procedure and Bankruptcy Law at Bocconi University and, since 2022, has served as the Head of its Department of Legal Studies. He is a member of the Board of Editors of the Rivista di Diritto Processuale and of Global Jurist. His expertise includes international and comparative civil procedure, Italian, European, and global bankruptcy law, and alternative and transnational dispute resolution.

[1] The event titled "Class Action and New Forms of Aggregate Litigation in the United States" was held at Bocconi University on May 10, 2024. The keynote address was delivered by Prof. Arthur Miller, with Prof. Helen Hershkoff as the discussant. The event

in the Legal Book Series published by Bocconi University Press, is of utmost importance. It aimed to explore access to civil justice from an international perspective, ensuring that legal scholars, law students, and professionals in civil justice all over the world feel included and part of a global legal community. The focus was on class actions as a specific form of aggregate litigation.

Arthur R. Miller and Helen Hershkoff's comprehensive presentations were preceded by welcoming remarks from Bocconi's Rector, Francesco Billari[2], and a joint introduction by Marta Cartabia and Cesare Cavallini. They emphasized the topic's relevance, timeliness, and the values underlying class actions. Their focus on the importance of class actions in the education of law students, which embraces both domestic and international perspectives, is a core mission of the Department of Legal Studies at Bocconi University, as enhanced by the Rector Francesco Billari. This emphasis on class actions as a crucial part of legal education is informative, inspiring, and motivating for future legal professionals, igniting a passion for their roles in the global legal community.

Class actions, as both a tool and a phenomenon of access to civil justice, represent the perfect intersection of private interests (protected rights) and public interests (methods of enforcing violated rights) within the framework of upholding constitutional principles of due

opened with welcome remarks from the Rector, Prof. Francesco Billari followed by an introduction by Prof. Cesare Cavallini and Prof. Marta Cartabia.

[2] Professor Francesco Candeloro Billari is Rector and Full Professor of Demography at Bocconi University. He was previously Head of the Sociology Department University of Oxford from 2012 to 2017 before returning to Bocconi. From 1999 to 2002, he was Head of the Independent Research Group on the Demography of Early Adulthood at the Max Planck Institute for Demographic Research. He has also served as President, Secretary-General, and Treasurer of the European Association for Population Studies. He is Editor-in-Chief of the scholarly journal Advances in Life Course Research, a position he has held since its inception in 2009. His expertise covers fertility and family change, the transition to adulthood, life course analysis, population forecasting, and agent-based modelling, among other topics in demography, economics, epidemiology and public health.

process. There could be no better way to learn about the origin and evolution of class actions than from the founders and advocates of civil liberties within the Anglo-American legal tradition. In the past decades, class actions have proven to be an effective instrument for giving voice to the voiceless in civil rights. Today, they stand ready to address in legal terms the significant challenges of our times related to the environment, the digital revolution, and inequalities, thereby demonstrating their historical, urgent, and contemporary significance.

Milan, September 2024

I   THE CLASS ACTION AND OTHER FORMS OF AGGREGATE LITIGATION IN THE UNITED STATES

*Professor Arthur R. Miller**

Thank you professors Cartabia and Cavallini for that very nice introduction. I must confess I am very proud that Queen Elizabeth II designated me a Commander of the Order of the British Empire. The only problem is, as my friends constantly remind me, the British don't have an empire anymore. Nevertheless, it comes with a nice medallion.

---

* University Professor and Warren E. Burger Professor of Constitutional Law and the Courts, NYU, School of Law, formerly Bruce Bromley Professor, Harvard Law School (1971 to 2007); faculty, Universities of Minnesota and Michigan. Undergraduate Degree, University of Rochester; J.D., Harvard Law School; Former Legal Editor, ABC's Good Morning America; Host, Miller's Court, and several other TV shows; National Emmy recipient for moderating *The Constitution: That Delicate Balance.* An author of numerous works on civil litigations, notably Wright & Miller, *Federal Practice and Procedure*; and on copyright and privacy issues. He also maintains an active law practice, particularly in the federal appellate courts. Among positions he has held are those of Commissioner on the United States Commission on New Technological Uses of Copyrighted Works, the Reporter for and then a Member of the Advisory Committee on Civil Rules of the Judicial Conference of the United States, and Reporter for the American Law Institute's Project on Complex Litigation. Miller's numerous awards include eight honorary doctorates, three American Bar Association Gavel Awards and a Special Gavel Award for promoting public understanding of the law. He was honored by Queen Elizabeth II for his charitable and media work who named him a Commander of the Order of the British Empire. Professor Miller spoke extemporaneously and has tried to preserve the conversational character of his presentations.

It is a special pleasure to be here. When I arrived, almost the first thing Professor Cavallini asked me was: have I ever been to Milan before? The answer is yes, I have. Indeed, my first trip to this part of Italy, in effect, began my public service activities when I was a young academic. Let me take you on a brief autobiographical trip through the history of when and why I was here and why the United States has embraced the class action and other forms of procedural aggregation. The year was 1961. My math is terrible, but I believe that is about 63 years ago. As I look around this room, I don't think many of you were here back then, but I was here. I had graduated from law school and practiced for a few years with a prominent New York law firm. I was making a transition into the academic world at Columbia Law School working on a major project focusing on what was then called International Judicial Assistance and determining whether I would be an effective teacher and like academia.

Those of you who will be practicing in the EU and beyond probably will come into contact with international judicial assistance because it often is needed when you are representing clients in litigation on matters involving cross-border activity. Let's suppose you are an Italian lawyer representing an Italian company in litigation involving conduct and people in several countries. Perhaps you need to serve process on someone in Switzerland or Japan. Or you want to take the testimony of a potential witness in the United States. Or, perhaps, prove the content of the relevant law of Saudi Arabia. Or you want to obtain official or private documents located in Brazil. Could you achieve these goals without the assistance of the judiciaries of these other countries?

It was a very avant-garde subject back then – most judicial systems did not assist each other in civil cases. There was little occasion for it. The limited existing procedures were clumsy and ineffective but cross-border litigation was relatively rare.

However, if one looked into the future it was clear that transnational litigation was increasing and there was a growing need for efficient procedures that would function beyond a particular forum's borders. The signs were there. To expand attention to the subject, the Columbia Project and interested people here in Italy organized a bilateral conference at a gorgeous villa near Varese. Italians and Americans at the highest level – jurists, practitioners, and scholars – were invited. Since I was the person at the Columbia Project who was drafting potential procedural rules and statutes to facilitate judicial assistance by courts in the United States and developing plans to encourage officials and proceduralists in other countries to do the same, I became a member of the American delegation.

The Conference was a heady experience for this youngster and enabled me to sample the beauty (and cuisine) of northern Italy. I especially remember a lovely boat trip for the delegates on Lago di Varese, which included stops to pay respects to judges in several communities around the lake. And, of course, there was time for several days here in Milan. My memories of these events are very good ones. Thus, my professional life in terms of activities and involvement in public policy issues really began just a few miles from here in 1961.

After the Varese conference I completed the drafting of several procedural rules to deal with the issues I mentioned and a possible statute empowering federal courts to assist litigants in foreign cases in the same manner as they would in domestic cases before them. The effort then turned to encouraging relevant people to consider the proposals. So I went to the Reporter of the Advisory Committee on Civil Rules of the Judicial Conference of the United States, – Harvard Law School Professor Benjamin Kaplan. That Committee is composed of distinguished judges and lawyers selected by the Chief Justice of the United States[1]. It studies the operation of and develops proposals to amend and improve the operations of the Federal Rules of Civil Procedure

I must confess, I thought I had an "in" with Ben. I had been his student and research assistant while in law school. He had become

---

[1] The rulemaking process for the federal courts is set out in 28 United States Code §§ 2702-74.

my mentor and I have revered him throughout my professional career[2]. He apparently had faith in my work ethic because he said: "I'll present your draft rules on International Judicial Assistance to the Advisory Committee, but you've got to agree to work with me on the Committee's current effort, the revision of all of the Federal Rules that govern the joinder of claims and joinder of parties"[3]. It was an offer I could not refuse[4]. I became his chief assistant, drafting proposed amendments to the Federal Rules of Civil Procedure for the Committee's consideration, which he would then, of course – as he always did with law school exams – extensively mark up with a red pencil. The most difficult work was revising the existing class action provision, Federal Rule 23[5].

---

[2] My reverence and gratitude to him is expressed in Arthur R. Miller, *In Memoriam: Benjamin Kaplan*, 124 Harv. L. Rev. 1345, 1354-57 (2011).

[3] As the Reporter, Ben would develop drafts of possible rule amendments and present them to the Advisory Committee which, if approved, then went through a lengthy and time-consuming evaluation by several other federal entities and eventually the Supreme Court. If the proposal successfully survived that process it became part of the Federal Rules and was applicable in all the Federal district courts. Years later I had the honor of serving the Committee, first as its Reporter and then as a Member. Many states have adopted all or some of the Federal Civil Rules for their courts.

[4] As promised, Ben submitted my International Judicial Assistance rule proposals to the Committee and allowed me to participate in its meetings, a thrilling experience. They eventually were approved by the Advisory Committee and successfully progressed through the other rulemaking entities and appear today as Federal Rule 4(f) (service of process), Rule 28(b) (depositions), Rule 44 (proof of an official record), and Rule 44.1 (determinination of foreign law) were approved. The proposed judicial assistance statute was presented to Congress and enacted into law as 28 United States Code § 1782. *See generally* 14B Charles A. Wright, Arthur R. Miller & Edward H. Cooper, Federal Practice and Procedure § 3692 (5th ed. 2023).

[5] My work with Professor Kaplan on the 1966 amendments is described in Arthur R. Miller, *Some Very Personal Reflections on the Rules, Rulemaking, and Reporters*, 46 U. Mich. J.L. Ref. 651 (2013). The Rule has been amended several times since 1966 largely to deal with certain aspects of class action practice.

That was my introduction to the class action. After going through many drafts and several Advisory Committee meetings, a new Rule 23 emerged[6], which journeyed through the rulemaking process and became effective in 1966. It is generally considered the keystone of the modern class action in the United States[7].

In many parts of the world the United States was criticized, sometimes rather sharply, for revising Federal Rule 23 the way it did in 1966. Some thought it was another example of American exceptionalism or a form of judicial imperialism as many class actions involve some class members who are not Americans or foreign defendants or multi-national activities[8]. Other critics expressed the view that the right to a day in court was an individual personal right and should not be collectivized. And others expressed concern that meritless class actions would be used to harass companies into unwarranted settlements. I remember many years ago being chided at an international conference for advocating what the speaker referred to as an "uncontrollable, lawless procedure". On another occasion, the chief justice of a great country said to me, "we will have a class action over my dead body". Much has changed in recent years as more and more countries increase their receptivity to the aggregation of civil claims

---

[6] A very extensive discussion of federal class actions is found in 7A Charles A. Wright, Arthur R. Miller, Mary Kay Kane & Robert H. Klonoff, Federal Practice and Procedure §§ 1751–1807 (4th ed. & Supp. 2024).

[7] With the enactment in 2005 of the Class Action Fairness Act (CAFA), 28 United States Code §§ 1332(d), 1453, all sizable class actions now are commenced in or are removed from state courts to the federal courts. *See* Standard Fire Insurance Co. v. Knowles, 568 U.S. 588 (2013). Rule 23 applies to CAFA cases. *See generally* 7A Charles A. Wright, Arthur R. Miller, Mary Kay Kane & Robert H. Klonoff, Federal Practice and Procedure § 1756.2 (4th ed. & Supp. 2024). Many states had a very active class action practice prior to CAFA.

[8] The Supreme Court has restricted this tendency in recent years by requiring a connection between the challenged conduct and the United States. *E.g.*, Morrison v. National Australia Bank Ltd., 561 U.S. 247 (2010) (fraud provisions of Securities Exchange Act limited to transactions on domestic exchanges).

in one form or another and nations as different as Brazil and Israel have class action procedures[9].

Of course, until recently, Italy was among the many countries without a wide-angle aggregation procedure, let alone a significant class action. Italy did not recognize the class action in a meaningful form until about 2021[10]. which has been amended several times since then[11]. It is not a class action American style. That's ok. But I do not think Italy's present procedure is as useful as it could be. I don't mean to be too critical, or an ungracious guest in your country. Rather I believe in and think Federal Rule 23 reflects some positive aspects of the civil justice system and the legal culture in my country. I think the same could be true in Italy.

Let me explain why so much attention was paid to the class action by the rulemaking process that led to the 1966 amendment. What motivated the complete revision of Federal Rule 23? Let me put it

---

[9] *See generally* Deborah R. Hensler, *From Sea to Shining Sea: How and Why Class Actions Are Spreading Globally*, 65 U. KAN. L. REV. 965, 986 (2017).

[10] Although the class action technically was introduced in Italy in 2007, that law had limited practical applicability because it only allowed aggregation in consumer rights suits; it also hindered litigants' ability to advertise the existence of the class, and it had stringent requirements for class eligibility. *See* Cecilia Buresti & Lucia Salerno, *Class Action Reform in Italy*, NORTON ROSE FULBRIGHT (June 2019), https://www.nortonrosefulbright.com/en-us/knowledge/publications/aac4cf20/class-action-reform-in-italy. The 2021 legislation allows class action suits in non-consumer cases and increased the number of laws under which a class action suit can be brought. *See* Boso Caretta, Massimo D'Andrea & Bice Di Sano, *New Italian Class Action Regime Enters into Force*, DLA PIPER (May 25, 2021), https://www.dlapiper.com/en-us/insights/publications/2021/05/new-italian-class-action-regime-enters-into-force.

[11] Recent amendments allow for cross-border class actions, enables the class action to seek both compensatory and inhibitory damages, and provides the procedural means to request both types of remedy simultaneously. *See* Tecla Maria Tunin & Emanuele Inturrisi, *The Italian Class Actions and Recent European Regulatory Developments*, RÖDL & PARTNER (Sept. 4, 2023), https://www.roedl.com/insights/european-regulatory-recent-developments-italian-class-actions.

in perspective. Certainly, neither the class action nor its underlying concept was born in the United States at that time. The fundamental philosophy and objectives of Rule 23 can be traced back to 1789; indeed, they existed even before the American Revolution in a number of the colonies[12]. The United States inherited the procedure from the British; it was part of their equity practice[13]. There is some evidence that the British didn't create it either, that it actually had emerged earlier in Scandinavia or possibly Germany[14]. No one really knows, and it doesn't matter anymore. The point is that the concept – a dispute can be litigated by aggregating people with similar claims into a group and allowing them to proceed on a collective basis – is centuries old. The existing Federal Rule was simply *amended* in 1966, albeit very extensively[15]. It was controversional and some people in

---

[12] The Supreme Court has long acknowledged the class action's roots in foundational constitutional principles and protections. *See, e.g.*, Amchem Prods., Inc. v. Windsor, 521 U.S. 591 (1997) (settlement class actions must meet Rule 23 requirements to ensure constitutionality); Phillips Petroleum Co. v. Shutts, 472 U.S. 797 (1985) (the Constitution's Due Process Clause mandates adequate representation, notice, and an opt-out option for class members in money actions); Eisen v. Carlisle v. Jacquelin, 417 U.S. 156 (1974) (individual notice of the action must be given to identifiable class members); Hansberry v. Lee, 311 U.S. 32 (1940) (adequate representation requirement is mandated by the Fourteenth Amendment). Class actions are an exception to the traditional rule that only actual parties to a suit are bound by the judgment. Taylor v. Sturgell. 553 U.S. 880 (2008).

[13] The development from the English Bill of Peace to the contemporary United States class action is set out in Stephen C. Yeazell, From Medieval Group Litigation to the Modern Class Action (1987). *See also* 1 Basil Montagu, Digest of Pleading in Equity (London, J. & W.T. Clarke 1824). Modern federal courts continue to recognize the equitable roots of the class action. *E.g.*, Ortiz v. Fibreboard Corp., 527 U.S. 815, 831 (1999). *See also* Stephen Subrin, *How Equity Conquered Common Law*, 135 U. Pa. L. Rev. 909 (1987).

[14] *See* Yeazell, note 13 above.

[15] Much of the history of the process that produced the 1966 revision of Rule 23 is told in John K. Rabiej, *The Making of Class Action Rule 23 – What Were We Thinking?*, 24 Miss. C. L. Rev. 323, 333–45 (2005). *See generally* 7A Charles A. Wright, Arthur R. Miller, Mary Kay Kane & Robert H. Klonoff,

the United States still have reservations about certain applications of the amended Rule[16].

The need to amend Rule 23 began to become apparent in 1954 when the United States Supreme Court declared segregated public education unconstitutional in *Brown v. Board of Education* – some of you know this part of American history[17]. Following that decision a flood of cases were commenced in communities throughout the United States seeking the desegregation of schools. The Advisory Committee on Civil Rules concluded that the federal courts could not handle this litigation effectively by proceeding one parent, one child, or even one school at a time. When the class action was suggested as a potential vehicle for facilitating the desegregation cases it was apparent that the existing Rule 23 was too archaic and its text was almost incomprehensible – it was unworkable.

Moreover, it seemed certain that the civil rights movement, which

---

FEDERAL PRACTICE AND PROCEDURE §§ 1777–84.1, 1804–05 (4th ed. & Supp. 2024); David Marcus, *The History of the Modern Class Action, Part I: Sturm and Drang*, 1953-1980, 74 WASH. U. L. REV. 587 (2013); Samuel Issacharoff & Peter Zimroth, *An Oral History of Rule 23: An Interview of Professor Arthur R. Miller*, 74 N.Y.U. ANN. SURV. AM. L. 105 (2018).

[16] *See, e.g.*, MARTIN H. REDISH, WHOLESALE JUSTICE: CONSTITUTIONAL DEMOCRACY AND THE PROBLEM OF THE CLASS ACTION LAWSUIT (2009); Myriam Gilles, *Opting Out of Liability: The Forthcoming Near-Total Demise of the Modern Class Action*, 104 MICH. L. REV. 373, 375 (2005); Linda S. Mullenix, *Ending Class Actions As We Know Them: Rethinking the American Class Action*, 64 EMORY L.J. 399 (2014). *See also* Arthur R. Miller, *Keynote Address: The American Class Action: From Birth to Maturity*, 19 THEORETICAL INQUIRIES IN LAW 1, 6 (2018) (explaining that some Advisory Committee members opposed the proposal to extend the Rule 23 class action because they disagreed with binding dispersed absent people with no prior nexus to each other); Robert H. Klonoff, *Class Action Part II: A Respite from the Decline*, 92 N.Y.U. L. REV. 971 (2017); Arthur R. Miller, *The Preservation and Rejuvenation of Aggregate Litigation: A Systemic Imperative*, 64 EMORY L.J. 293 (2014); Symposium, *Class Actions and Access to Justice*, 82 GEO. WASH. L. REV. 595 (2004).

[17] Brown v. Bd. of Educ. of Topeka, Kan., 347 U.S. 483, 873 (1954). *Brown* actually was not a class action; it was a consolidation of cases from five different jurisdictions but had all the trappings of a class action.

had become very active by the early 1960's, was not going to limit its challenges to cases seeking desegregation of educational facilities for people of color[18]. Civil Rights lawyers certainly were going to attack segregated interstate transportation facilities, water fountains, and public bathrooms, as well as assert the right of people to sit on a bus or train or an assplane where they wanted[19]. In addition, one could predict that the movement would be carried forward by other marginalized groups, not just people of color[20]. There inevitably were going to be cases involving gender discrimination[21]. In time, there would be

---

[18] Civil rights legislation was submitted to the House of Representatives' Rules Committee in November of 1963, which became the Civil Rights Act of 1964, Pubic Law No. 88-352, 78 Stat. 241 (codified as 42 United States Code §§ 2000e *et seq.*), and the Voting Rights Act of 1965, Public Law. 89-110, 79 Stat. 43 (codified as 52 United States Code §§ 10301 *et seq.*), was enacted the following year. This was a period in which the Congress enacted many statutes protecting citizens and advancing public policies.

As my colleague Professor Hershkoff explores in her paper, pages 37-45 and elsewhere, *see, e.g.,* Helen Hershkoff & Luke Norris, *The Oligarchic Courthouse: Jurisdiction, Corporate Power, and Democratic Decline,* 122 MICH. L. REV. 1 (2023), the United States, particularly its federal judicial system, is in a far more restrictive mood today with regard to various constitutional protections and civil rights. *See, e.g.,* Students for Fair Admissions, Inc. v. President and Fellows of Harvard College, 600 U.S. 181 (2023) (eliminating the use of race in college admissions); Dobbs v. Jackson Women's Health Organization, 597 U.S. 2115 (2022) (overriding the constitutional right to abortion recognized by the Supreme Court in Roe v. Wade, 410 U.S. 113 (1973)).

[19] *See* 7A CHARLES A. WRIGHT, ARTHUR R. MILLER, MARY KAY KANE & ROBERT H. KLONOFF, FEDERAL PRACTICE AND PROCEDURE §§ 1776–76.1 (4th ed. & Supp. 2024) (explaining the role of class actions in protecting a variety of civil and constitutional rights).

[20] *See, e.g.,* Gilmore v. City of Montgomery, Ala., 417 U.S. 556 (1974); Norwood v. Harrison, 413 U.S. 455 (1973); Griffin v. County School Board, 377 U.S. 218 (1964).

[21] *See, e.g.,* Wal-Mart Stores, Inc. v. Dukes, 564 U.S. 338 (2011); United Automobile Workers v. Johnson Controls, 499 U.S. 187 (1991); Manning v. Int'l Union, 466 F.2d 812 (6th Cir. 1972), cert. denied, 410 U.S. 946 (1973).

cases seeking equal facilities for the disabled, and then, my personal favorite, there would be cases involving age discrimination[22]. The Advisory Committee on Civil Rules I mentioned earlier therefore agreed to rewrite and modernize Rule 23 to create a functionable procedural vehicle that could be used in a wide array of civil rights cases[23]. That was the first motivation that led to the 1966 revision of Rule 23.

Beyond that, the Committee felt there was an obvious and very practical objective that led to the revision: why should the federal courts be burdened by what essentially were the same or closely related cases or superintend the same deposition or document discovery hundreds or possibly thousands of times in individual cases when it could be done once in a single master case? The federal courts don't have the judicial resources to adjudicate numerous related – let alone closely related – claims one by one by one. The Committee understood that the judicial system, given its limited resources had to take advantage of the efficiency and economy of aggregation. Even by the earlier 1960's it was apparent that the federal courts and the parties simply cannot afford expensive and time-consuming repetitive dispursed individual adjudications with its risks of different procedural treatment and inconsistent results. Thus a desire for litigation efficiency and economy coupled with a desire for consistency of results provided a second motivation for the Advisory Committee's considerable attention to the potential utility of class actions that led to the 1966 revision of Rule 23.

A third motivation was somewhat less obvious at the time of the Rule's revision but has been recognized over the years as a central

---

[22] *See, e.g.*, Fed. Express Corp. v. Holowecki, 552 U.S. 389 (2008); Hoffmann-La Roche v. Sperling, 493 U.S. 165 (1989); Basch v. Ground Round, Inc., 139 F.3d 6 (1st Cir. 1998).

[23] The Advisory Committee also understood that a new, more user-friendly, Rule could prove effective in a wide range of civil rights cases and possibly actions under several federal remedial statutes, such as the antitrust or securities laws. Arthur R. Miller, *Keynote Address: The American Class Action: From Birth to Maturity*, 19 Theoretical Inquiries in Law 1, 5 (2018).

objective of aggregation. Indeed, it is reflected in what Professor Cavallini said earlier this morning and is echoed in his co-authored Forward with Professor Cartabia, the need to increase access to civil justice. As my mentor argued to the Advisory Committee members at several meetings it is essential to have an aggregation procedure that enables economically disadvantaged people – indeed, disadvantaged people of all kinds – or those with modest means – to combine their limited resources and bring an economically viable collective lawsuit against companies the size of Exxon or Microsoft, or any other powerful entity[24]. How else can disadvantaged people possibly litigate effectively against an enormous corporation, let alone the government? In other words, the class action was perceived by a majority of the Committee as an access-to-justice mechanism that gives people without sufficient resources or a substantial enough claim to attract talented counsel who cannot afford to litigate on an individual basis against a powerful entity, the ability to have their grievances presented by adequately incentivizing attorneys economically to undertake collective representation. In short, Rule 23 was rewritten to increase access to the federal courts' civil justice system. That was a third motivation for the 1966 revision of the class action rule.

There is an important aspect of the American litigation scene that should be understood in connection with this third motivation. There are many lawyers in the United States. Many people would say too many. Most lawyers are paid by the hour, and talented lawyers have hourly rates that are very high. Realistically an individual lawyer or small firm is at a distinct disadvantage in a contest against multibillion-dollar companies or anyone who is very wealthy, regarding any manner likely to be protracted or expensive to pursue and would be

---

[24] The Advisory Committee's Reporter and many members of the Committee wanted the new Rule 23 to be flexible and able to function beyond the existing class action boundaries, including allowing the aggregation of small claims that realistically could not be brought individually. Benjamin Kaplan, *A Prefatory Note, The Class Action – A Symposium*, 10 B.C. INDUS. & COM. L. REV. 497, 497 (1969).

very reluctant to undertake such a venture on behalf of an individual client. Even if there were a lawyer who would take on such a case, almost no individual, or even groups of individuals, could afford to pay that lawyer by the hour. I estimate that 90 percent to 95 percent of Americans cannot pay what gifted and effective lawyers charge on an hourly basis or advance funds for the expenses of litigation.

That is why a long time ago, the right to compensate lawyers on a contingent basis was generally recognized in the United States: a practice that is not acceptable in most countries. Indeed, in some countries it is thought of as a form of gambling, or partnering with the client, which is professionally inappropriate and subject to restrictions and sanctions. A contingent fee system avoids requiring prospective plaintiffs to pay fees or even reimburse expenses on an upfront or hourly basis. The lawyer is compensated, and expenses reimbursed, only if he or she is successful on recovering something for the client. I personally believe that the ability to retain a lawyer on a contingency basis is an extremely significant access-to-civil-justice mechanism that is particularly valuable in the class action context[25].

In my experience, plaintiffs' lawyers are a hardy bunch – they are risk assumptive. They often take on seemingly hopeless or small claim cases, sometimes for socially desirable objectives, and are will-

---

[25] Additionally, there is an old common law principle that a fee can be awarded to lawyers who produce a common benefit for all the class members. *See, e.g.,* Boeing Co. v. Van Gemert, 444 U.S. 472 (1980); Trustees v. Greenough, 105 U.S. 527 (1881). The attorney fee shifting provisions in many statutes and the general acceptance of the common fund fee sharing principle make the class action attractive to plaintiffs' lawyers. *See* 7B CHARLES A. WRIGHT, ARTHUR R. MILLER & MARY KAY KANE, FEDERAL PRACTICE AND PROCEDURE §§ 1803–1803.2 (3d ed. & Supp. 2024). This doctrine, however, is of limited application when the claim is seeking purely injunctive or declaratory relief. *See, e.g.,* Alyeska Pipeline Serv. Co. v. Wilderness Society, 421 U.S. 240 (1975). Another economic aspect of litigation in the United States is that there are no loser-pay rules regarding litigation expenses; litigation costs are left with the party that incurred them absent a statute to the contrary.

ing to do so on a contingent basis and assume the risks of non-compensation and non-reimbursement[26]. Also many of the lawyers who typically represent people on the plaintiffs' side of the "v" are aggressive or at least tenacious by nature. These characteristics coupled with the contingent fee create realistic litigation risks for substantial defendants and go a long way toward opening the courthouse doors for people and leveling the litigation playing field[27].

After the revised Rule 23 went into effect, perhaps for at least 10 years, it was used extensively to challenge racial segregation. In many major cities in the United States, the public schools were ordered desegregated, as were public water fountains, toilets, and transportation facilities. Then, as many predicted, utilization of the 1966 Rule began to widen: a wave of gender discrimination cases were brought by women who claimed they either were denied employment or were discriminated against in terms of employment conditions, such as salary or promotion or both[28].

---

[26] An addition to the risk of not receiving any compensation if the action fails, any monies expended by a plaintiff's lawyer for litigation expenses cannot be recovered from the client absent a contractual basis for doing so. These expenses can be very substantial if extensive discovery, expert testimony, or scientific testing of a product is needed.

[27] In federal and most state courts attorneys' fees and reimbursement of costs in a successful class action are set by the court, not the lawyers, following a proceeding, which often is adversarial and extensive, that is subject to objection and review on appeal. *See, e.g.,* Federal Rule 23(h). Most court awarded fees reflect the quality of the result achieved for the class and the risks inherent in contingent fee representation. *See generally* 7B CHARLES A. WRIGHT, ARTHUR R. MILLER & MARY KAY KANE, FEDERAL PRACTICE AND PROCEDURE §§ 1803–03.2 (3d ed. & Supp. 2024). It is the judge's responsibility to make certain the fees and expenses are reasonable.

[28] *See, e.g.,* Wal-Mart Stores, Inc. v. Dukes, 564 U.S. 338 (2011) (alleging that the company's pay and promotion practices allegedly disproportionately favored men); Sheehan v. Purolator, Inc., 839 F.2d 99 (2d Cir. 1988) (challenging pay disparities between male and female employees). *See also* 7A CHARLES A. WRIGHT, ARTHUR R. MILLER, MARY KAY KANE & ROBERT H. KLONOFF, FED-

Beyond race and gender discrimination, Rule 23 became the procedural vehicle for seeking enforcement by injunction and declaratory relief of a wide range of constitutional rights and challenging various governmental practices[29]. Earlier Professor Cavallini referred to "due process," a right with a broad scope that all Americans are guaranteed by the Fifth and Fourteenth Amendments to our Constitution, including people in prison. Thus, litigation involving various prison conditions became the subject of class action litigation[30].

In due course some contingent fee lawyers' reached the logical conclusion that if the class action could be used for protecting civil and constitutional rights, it also must be employable for antitrust, securities, and other claims having a public purpose seeking monetary relief for injured individuals. Slowly but surely, the courts began to accept the use of the class action in those cases[31]. Not surprisingly, lawyers then concluded that if Rule 23 could be used in these categories, it must be available to remedy product failures, defective tires on cars,

---

ERAL PRACTICE AND PROCEDURE §§ 1776–76.1 (4th ed. & Supp. 2024) (discussing the applicability of the class action in civil and constitutional rights contexts).

[29] *Id. See also* Johnson v. City of Arcadia, Florida, 450 F.Supp. 1363 (M.D. Fla. 1978) (municipal service access); Thompson v. Bond, 421 F. Supp. 878 (W.D. Mo. 1976) (challenging a state's civil-death statute); Stewart v. Waller, 404 F.Supp. 206 (N.D. Miss. 1975) (voting rights). This theme will be pursued in greater detail by Professor Hershkoff.

[30] For example, in Brown v. Plata, 563 U.S. 493 (2011), California prisoners with serious mental and physical conditions brought a class action against the Governor of California alleging that due to prison overcrowding, they received inadequate health care, violating their Eighth Amendment right to be free of "cruel and unusual punishments." The district court ordered the state to formulate a plan to reduce the state's prison population and submitted it for court approval. The Supreme Court held that the court-mandated population limit was necessary to remedy the overcrowding.

[31] *See, e.g.,* Tellabs, Inc. v. Makor Issues & Rts., Ltd., 551 U.S. 308, 313 (2007) (securities fraud); In re Amgen Inc. Sec. Litig., 544 F. Supp. 2d 1009, 1022 (C.D. Cal. 2008) (securities fraud).

toasters that explode, or mislabeled consumer products[32], as well as cases under a variety of other statutes or common law principles serving public purposes[33]. Others naturally ventured further, thinking if the class action works in all of these contexts, well, why shouldn't it work for injuries from toxic substances and injurious pharmaceuticals? After all, not every pill prescribed by a doctor is pharmacologically sound. So class actions expanded into pharmaceuticals and from that into medical devices, prosthetics, toxic substances[34], and environmental contaminants[35]. The rationale was that these are all very significant areas of public policy that should be supported by private litigation seeking both monetary and specific relief.

That is how and why the United States developed the class action and other aggregation procedures. Looking back at this history, it tells a story that reflects a common pattern in the operation of the American civil justice system as well as the common law process. A new procedural rule with general language that many thought was primarily designed for race-based civil rights cases proves to be employable by creative lawyers and applicable by judges exercising wide discretion and management authority to meet societal needs in unanticipated ways that surprise many. I remember periodically visiting my mentor in the years after I had joined the Harvard Law School

---

[32] *See, e.g.,* Butler v. Sears Roebuck & Co., 727 F.3d 796 (7th Cir. 2012), cert denied, 571 U.S. 1196 (2014) (defective washing machines); Briseno v. ConAgra Foods, Inc., 844 F.3d 1121 (9th Cir. 2017), cert. denied, 583 U.S. 914 (2017) (false and misleading labelling).

[33] *See, e.g.,* Tyson Foods, Inc. v. Bouaphakeo, 577 U.S. 442 (2016) (Fair Labor Standards Act).

[34] *See, e.g.,* Amchem Prods., Inc. v. Windsor, 521 U.S. 51, 59 (1997) (current and future asbestos exposure); Ortiz v. Fibreboard Corp., 527 U.S. 815 (1999) (asbestos); In re National Prescription Opiate Litigation, 976 F.3d 664 (6th Cir. 2020) (opioids); Castano v. Am. Tobacco Co., 84 F.3d 734, 737 (5th Cir. 1996) (nicotine and tobacco products); Sterling v. Velsical Chem. Corp., 856 F. 2d 1188 (6th Cir. 1988), cert denied, 490 U.S. 1027 (1989) (chemical waste).

[35] Mejdrech v. Met-Coil Sys. Corp., 319 F. 3d 910 (7th Cir. 2002).

faculty and he had become a member of the Massachusetts Supreme Judicial Court. Ben would always ask me: "What's happening to our rule?" And I would respond, "you wouldn't believe how it is being used". And, on occasion, it was hard to convince him that the evolution I have just described was taking place.

Forgive me if I take a brief detour at this point. I do so because it is important to highlight that the class action is not the only aggregation procedure in the United States. Two years after the 1966 revision of Federal Rule 23, another form of aggregation was created by Congress – Multidistrict Litigation (MDL)[36]. In essence, the MDL statute creates a special tribunal – the Judicial Panel on Multidistrict Litigation – of seven federal judges (all appointed by the Chief Justice) and empowers it to transfer significantly similar related federal cases to a single judge for pretrial proceedings[37]. The resulting procedure is a form of consolidation and aggregation, similar in many ways to the class action but different as well in some key respects[38]. Once the pretrial proceedings are concluded on a collective basis, the individual cases in the consolidated MDL are returned to their courts of origination for further proceedings[39].

---

[36] See 28 United States Code § 1407. See generally 15 Charles A. Wright, Arthur R. Miller, Edward H. Cooper & Richard D. Freer, Federal Practice and Procedure, §§ 3861–68 (4th ed. 2013); Andrew Bradt, A Radical Proposal: The Multidistrict Litigation Act of 1968, 165 U. Pa. L. Rev. 831 (2017).

[37] The MDL statute allows for all "civil actions involving one or more common questions of fact" located in any federal district court in the Nation to be consolidated and transferred for pretrial proceedings. A number of states now have procedures for transferring related cases to one court in that state analogous to the federal MDL.

[38] See generally Robert H. Klonoff, Federal Multidistrict Litigation in a Nutshell 30–35 (2020).

[39] See Lexicon, Inc. v. Milberg Weiss Bershad Hynes & Lerach, 523 U.S. 26 (1998). The vast majority of MDL's are terminated in the transferee court by consent, dismissal, settlement, or summary judgment. See Elizabeth Chamblee Burch, Monopolies in Multidistrict Litigation, 70 Vand. L. Rev. 67 (2017) (the author estimates that only 2.9% of cases are retransferred to their original court).

The MDL has become a very common alternative to the class action and has become a major federal litigation phenomenon, often praised for increasing the efficient utilization of judicial resources and reducing procedural duplication particularly with regard to discovery. But MDL aggregation has come under considerable scrutiny for lacking some of the procedural safeguards provided for in class actions, or promoting over-centralization, and being relatively unclear in terms of the duties and powers of the transferee judge and the lawyers appointed by that judge to lead the collectivized cases[40]. Indeed, some believe that the MDL effectively has become a procedure designed to promote settlements[41].

When one considers aggregation in the United States, the reality is that the MDL is now more common and in some respects more important than the class action[42]. Moreover, in a few instances bankruptcy has been employed, not always successfully, as an alter-

---

[40] *See generally* ELIZABETH CHAMBLEE BURCH, MASS TORT DEALS: BACKROOM BARGAINING IN MULTIDISTRICT LITIGATION (2019) (discussing, among other things, the lack of MDL procedural guardrails and the tendency of MDL cases to be brought and managed by a few select plaintiffs' attorneys). In a number of cases, district judges have filled the gaps in the MDL statute by employing established class action procedures by analogy, typically regarding the approval of settlement and setting attorney fees. *See, e.g.,* In re Zyprexa Products Liability Litigation, 433 F. Supp. 2d 268 (E.D.N.Y. 2006); In re Guidant Corp. Implantable Defibrillators Products Liab. Litigation, 2008 WL 682174, at *19 (D. Minn. 2008). The resulting case is often referred to as a "quasi class action". *See also* the discussion in note 54, below.

[41] *See generally* RICHARD NAGREDA, MASS TORTS IN A WORLD OF SETTLEMENT (2007); Harold M. Erichson & Benjamin C. Zipursky, *Consent Closure,* 96 CORNELL L. REV. 265 (2011).

[42] MDLs have become more popular among plaintiff lawyers in part because the class action requirements have become increasingly exacting making the certification process time-consuming and highly risky. *See* Eldon E. Fallon, *Common Benefit Fees in Multidistrict Litigation,* 74 LA. L. REV. 371, 372–73 (2014); Robert H. Klonoff, *The Decline of Class Actions,* 90 WASH. U. L. REV. 729, 745–55 (2013).

native form of aggregation to both the class action and an MDL[43]. As is developed in Professor Hershkoff's paper, there are procedural formats that are not actually aggregate in form but have that effect in operation. These include actions by state attorneys general on behalf of all citizens of the state (*parens patriae* actions), the national injunction sought by an individual citizen that will benefit people similarly situation throughout the country, actions for the benefit of the state brought by a private individual for an injury to the state (*qui tam* actions)[44]. There are others.

Finally, mention should be made that to counteract the litigation opportunities aggregation offers plaintiffs and the considerable risks large-scale aggregations pose to defense interests, many companies have resorted to inserting mandatory arbitration clauses in contracts, particularly consumer and employment contracts that specifically prohibit the use of any aggregation procedure, thereby limiting plaintiffs to bringing their claims individually in arbitration, which will be economically or practically impossible for most people[45]. To

---

[43] *See* Harrington v. Purdue Pharma L.P., 603 U.S. ---, 144 S. Ct. 2071 (2024); In re Combustion Engineering, 391 F. 3d 190 (3d Cir. 2004); In re Joint Eastern and Southern District Asbestos Litigation, 78 F.3d 764 (2d Cir. 1996). *See generally* Troy A. McKenzie, *Toward a Bankruptcy Model for Nonclass Aggregate Litigation*, 87 N.Y.U. L. REV. 960 (2012) (proposing bankruptcy as a viable alternative to the class action). Other aggregation techniques fall within a category of procedures collectively referred to as alternative dispute resolution.

[44] *See* Hershkoff, at pages 45-53. *See generally* Myriam E. Gilles & Gary Friedman, *The New Qui Tam: A Model for the Enforcement of Group Rights in a Hostile Era*, 98 TEX. L. REV. 489 (2020); Suzette M. Malveaux, *Class Actions, Civil Rights, and the National Injunction*, 131 HARV. L. REV. F. 56 (2017); Michael Sant'Ambrogio & Adam S. Zimmerman, *Inside the Agency Class Action*, 131 YALE L.J. 1634 (2017).

[45] Partially in recognition of the economic threat to corporations of large scale class actions and MDL's, the Supreme Court has upheld the use of arbitration clauses, which *ex ante* contract away the rights of consumers and employees to seek judicial remedies in any aggregated format, thereby limiting them to bringing their claims individually in arbitration. The Court has done this in the past

meet this obstacle, some plaintiffs' lawyers have "bundled together a large number of individual arbitration demands to produce a single collective arbitration; whether this technique will prove to be successful remains to be seen[46].

Now let me proceed with both the class action and the MDL in mind. Both can be employed in any substantive context. Neither the language of the 1966 Federal Rule 23 nor the 1968 MDL statute are restricted to any substantive category, they are wide angle in scope; it does not matter what the underlying claim or sought-after relief is. But the federal court house door is not always wide open. Far from it. Every aggregation request must satisfy each of the demanding prerequisites for class certification set out in Federal Rule 23 before the court will certify it to proceed as a class action or convince the MDL court that collectivization and transfer are warranted[47]. Many

fifteen years despite contrary state law or important federal policies. *See, e.g.,* American Express Co. v. Italian Colors Restaurant, 570 U.S. 228 (2013); AT&T Mobility LLC v. Concepcion, 563 U.S. 333 (2011); *See also* Lamps Plus, Inc. v. Varela, 584 U.S. 959 (2018); Epic Systems Corp. v. Lewis, 584 U.S. 497 (2018). For an in-depth discussion of this phenomenon and its implications, see JACK H. FRIEDENTHAL, MARY KAY KANE, ARTHUR R. MILLER & ADAM N. STEINMAN, CIVIL PROCEDURE § 17.2 (6th ed. 2021). *See generally* Arthur R. Miller, *Simplified Pleading, Meaningful Days in Court, and Trials on the Merits: Reflections on the Deformation of Federal Procedure,* 88 N.Y.U. L. REV. 286, 323-31 (2013).

[46] *See generally* J. Maria Glover, *Mass Arbitration,* 75 STAN. L. REV. 1283 (2022); Cheryl Wilson, *Mass Arbitration: How the Newest Frontier of Mandatory Arbitration Jurisprudence Has Created a New Private Enforcement Regime in the Gig Economy Era,* 69 UCLA L. REV. 372 (2022).

[47] Fed. R. Civ. P. 23(a); these requirements are discussed in detail in 7A CHARLES A. WRIGHT, ARTHUR R. MILLER, MARY KAY KANE & ROBERT H. KLONOFF, FEDERAL PRACTICE AND PROCEDURE §§ 1759–71 (4th ed. & Supp. 2024) and 7AA CHARLES A. WRIGHT, ARTHUR R. MILLER, MARY KAY KANE & ROBERT H. KLONOFF, FEDERAL PRACTICE AND PROCEDURE §§ 1772-84.1 (4th ed. & Supp. 2024). The class must satisfy all the requirements in Rule 23(a) and fall within one of the three class action categories described in Rule 23(b)). The Supreme Court has directed the lower federal courts to enforce all of these prerequisites "rigorously". *See, e.g.,* Wal-Mart Stores, Inc. v. Dukes, 554 U.S.

cases, particularly in the personal injury context do not qualify for one reason or another[48].

And keep in mind that class actions, as well as under Rule 23 on the MDL statute, particularly those that are in any sense big or complex, subject to the highly developed culture in the United States federal courts of judicial management reflected in the Federal Rules[49] and well-developed judicial practices that give district judges who typically are assigned to cases for all purposes, the final determination throughout the proceeding on critical procedural issues such as the class definition, each of the Rule's requirements, the notice to be given to absent class members, the propriety of a proposed settlement, the structure and sequence of pretrial discovery and the trial, the administration of relief, and attorney fee and expense awards[50]. Many comparable practices have been developed in MDL practice by transferee judges[51].

---

338 (2011); General Telephone Co. of Southwest v. Falcon, 457 U.S. 147 (1982). These decisions reflect the Court's heavy reliance on judicial discretion and case management. See 7AA CHARLES A. WRIGHT, ARTHUR R. MILLER, MARY KAY KANE & ROBERT H. KLONOFF, FEDERAL PRACTICE AND PROCEDURE § 1784 (4th ed. & Supp. 2024).

[48] *See, e.g.,* TransUnion LLC v. Ramirez, 594 U.S. 413 (2021) (lack of standing); Amgen Inc. v. Connecticut Retirement Plans & Trust funds, 568 U.S. 455 (2013) (failure of proof of fraud on the market); Amchem Prods. Inc. v. Windsor, 521 U.S. 291 (1997) (lack of predominance of common questions); Gates v. Rohm & Haas Co., 655 F.3d 255 (3d Cir. 2011) (proposed class lacked cohesion).

[49] *See* Fed. R. Civ. P. 16, 23. *See generally* 6A CHARLES A. WRIGHT, ARTHUR R. MILLER & MARY KAY KANE, FEDERAL PRACTICE AND PROCEDURE §§ 1521-31 (3d ed. 2018).

[50] *See* Fed. R. Civ. P. 16, 23. *See, e.g.,* In re Southwest Airlines Voucher Litigation, 799 F.3d 700 (7th Cir. 2015) (settlement); Sullivan v. DB Investments, Inc., 667 F.3d 273 (7th Cir. 2011) (en banc) (class certification).

[51] Multidistrict litigation has not been subject to formal rule or statutory controls as 28 United States Code § 1407 does not contain any, but the same principles of judicial management set out in Federal Rule 16 apply to MDL's and some of the class action protections have been applied by analogy. *See, e.g.,* In re World trade Center Disaster Site Litigation, 754 F.3d 114 (2d Cir. 2014); In re Zyprexa

Almost no country has made the class action or other forms of aggregation universally available regardless of substantive or procedural context. Italy has not done so. It has compartmentalized the class action – in some contexts proceeding by representation is available, in some it is not[52]. In my judgment that is unnecessarily restrictive. The utility of the class action as well as other forms of aggregation is not limited to any particular substantive field or fields.

The other mistake I think Italy and the European Union have made, is that both have aggregation procedures that are opt-in in character. As a result, if someone wants to become a member of the class or group or association and benefit from or be bound by the result of the case, that person must affirmatively opt into the action[53]. That requirement undoubtedly will reduce the effectiveness of the resulting judgment, whether it is for or against the plaintiffs.

I remember the debates within the Federal Rules Advisory Committee in the early 1960's which considered this very subject on several occasions. Some members argued that a class action should benefit or be binding only on people who had signified a willingness to participate in the litigation as class members. A majority of the Committee, however, preferred to benefit and bind all those who fell within the class definition except those who chose to opt out of

---

Prods. Liability Litigation, 424 F. Supp. 3d 488 (E.D.N.Y. 2006); In re Guidant Corp. Implanted Defibrillators Prods. Liab. Litigation, 2008 WL 3896006 (D. Minn. 2008). That lack of procedural guidance in Section 1407 is about to be partially corrected because the current Rules Advisory Committee and the other rulemaking entities have adopted a new Federal Rule 16.1, largely modeled after existing Rule 16, dealing with certain aspects of MDL judicial management. If the Supreme Court approves the new Rule, as is expected, it will become effective as early as December 1, 2025.

[52] *See* note 53 below.

[53] *See* Directive 2020/1828 of the European Parliament and of the Council of 25 November 2020 on Representative Actions for the Protection of the Collective Interests of Consumers and Repealing Directive 2009/22/EC, 2020 O.J. (L 106).

an action seeking monetary relief under Federal Rule 23. The fear they expressed was that many people would not receive the class action notice, or would not read it, or would dispose of it the way most people treat what looks like junk mail. Moreover, these Committee members recognized that there are millions of people in the United States who are not literate in English or could not understand the notice's content even if they tried to read it. And, of course, this debate took place long before the internet. Thus, there was no way of communicating electronically with class members.

So the decision was made for the federal courts: everyone who is within the class definition is in the action. If a class member does not want to be in a case seeking monetary relief because he or she does not like lawyers or lawsuits are against that person's religious beliefs – whatever the reason might be – that member can opt out of the action and proceed against the defendant on his or her own, or do nothing[54]. But, a class member who remains silent will be bound by the class action judgment; that will be true, of course, only if the Rule 23 procedures and its protections have been honored[55].

Those of you who are Italian lawyers will have many occasions to think about the future of your Nation's (and the EU's) class action as well as other aggregation methodologies. When you do, consider whether these procedures are functioning effectively or should be amended to permit broader applicability of aggregation and greater protections for those who may be affected by collective procedures.

---

[54] In some contexts the claims of class members are so small it is unrealistic to expect individuals to take any action even if they read and understand the notice. *See* Benjamin Kaplan, *Continuing Work of the Civil Committee: 1966 Amendments of the Federal Rules of Civil Procedure (I)*, 81 HARV. L. REV. 356, 497-98 (1967) (requiring class members to opt-in would "freez[e] out. . . small claims").

[55] *See* Cooper v. Federal Reserve Bank of Richmond, 467 U.S. 867 (1984). An opt-out system thus gives the judgment greater binding effect than does an opt-in system and arguably produces efficiency, equality of treatment of class members, greater predictability, and more litigation peace for defendants. *See generally* Tobias B. Wolff, *Preclusion in Class Action Litigation*, 105 COLUM. L. REV. 717 (2005).

These questions involve social judgments; in some respects, of course, they are political or economic judgments.

I cannot say everything has gone beautifully regarding class actions in the United States since 1966. It hasn't. Defense interests have repeatedly disparaged Rule 23 and pressed for its revision and in recent decades a number of federal courts have rendered opinions that some would say have unduly restricted the application of class actions[56]. In recent decades the political shift to the right in the United States particularly with regard to the composition of the Supreme Court as the United States has moved from the Warren Court to the Burger, Rehnquist and Roberts Courts, has led to a more conservative federal judiciary with a more pro-business orientation[57]. That has led to judicial concern about intimidation by lawsuit and the consequences of getting an issue wrong in a single aggregated case.

Moreover, occasionally frivolous or marginal class actions are filed, some motivated by lawyers looking for the fee award that a settlement or a successful result might produce. One, in particular, comes to mind. I've only been in Italy for 5 days on this trip. Despite having looked around fairly carefully, I have yet to see a Subway sandwich

---

[56] *See* Wal-Mart Stores, NC. v. Dukes, 564 U.S. 338 (2011); Castano v. American Tobacco Co., 84 F.3d 734 (5th Cir. 2011); Matter of Rhone-Poulenc Rorer, Inc., 51 F.3d 1293 (7th Cir. 1995), cert denied, 516 U.S. 867 (1995). *See generally* Stephen Burbank & Sean Farhang, *Class Actions and the Counterrevolution Against Federal Litigation*, 165 U. PA. L. REV. 1495 (2017); Robert H. Klonoff, *Class Actions Part II: A Respite from the Decline*, 92 N.Y.U. L. REV. 971, 972, 976 (2017). The early days of the class action debate are discussed in Arthur R. Miller, *Of Frankenstein Monsters and Shining Knights, Myth, Reality, and the Class Action Problem*, 92 HARV. L. REV. 664 (1979).

[57] Several prominent scholars have noted and criticized this shift because it has reduced the availability of Rule 23 class actions, particularly in rights oriented litigation. *See, e.g.,* Owen M. Fiss, *Foreword: The Forms of Justice*, 93 HARV. L. REV. 1 (1979); Robert H. Klonoff, *The Decline of Class Actions*, 90 WASH. U. L. REV. 729 (2013); Edward A. Purcell, Jr., *The Class Action Fairness Act in Perspective: The Old and the New in Federal Jurisdictional Reform*, 156 U. PA. L. REV. 1823 (2008).

shop. I have seen Burger King and McDonald's and other fast-food places I recognize. Many of you know the Subway chain; it is global and everywhere it offers what it calls the "footlong" sandwich. "The Subway Footlong". Apparently, that has been a highly successful sales pitch.

A class action was brought on behalf of Subway consumers claiming the sandwiches were not a foot long[58]. They were shorter, it was alleged, perhaps only 11 or $11^{1/2}$ inches long. Frankly, I don't wish cases like that on any of you! What is that case worth to each class member – perhaps 3 or 6 cents or a bit more for each sandwich for those customers who could show proof of purchase and injury.

I frequently ask students, what are courts for? Certainly they should seek to deter misconduct and compensate victims. So assuming for the moment that the allegations were proven, that would be fraud which should be stopped and others deterred from similar conduct even if an individual's damages were only 3 or 6 cents per sandwich. Obviously no case on behalf of one individual would ever be brought even if the plaintiff could show the purchase of a hundred sandwiches and the defendant's conduct warranted punitive damages – that claim is economically unviable for both the consumer and the lawyer. However, if there were thousands or millions of consumers in a "Footlong" class and you could aggregate 3 to 6 cents a sandwich plus punitive damages and a substantial attorneys' fee, it might lead to a substantial monetary recovery and produce a good deal of deterrence. So the case initially appeared plausible to some even if it seemed somewhat silly.

Unfortunately, when the facts emerged, it turned out the sandwiches almost always were a foot long. Any variations probably were

---

[58] The district court approved a settlement for injunctive relief plus attorney's fees of $520,000 and incentive fees of $5,000 for the actual plaintiffs. In re Subway Footlong Sandwich Mktg. & Sales Practices Litig., 316 F.R.D. 240 (E.D. Wis. 2016). An objector appealed and the court of appeals reversed and ordered the case dismissed, 869 F.3d 551 (7th Cir. 2017).

the result of the baking process. It was an embarrassing moment for the class action[59]. Yes, sadly we do get a few cases like that. Fortunately, the judicial discretion and management techniques provided for in several of the Federal Rules of Civil Procedure and elsewhere in federal practice enable judges who understand they have a gate-keeper function to identify and dismiss cases lacking procedural and substantive merit as soon as that becomes obvious[60].

Let me now take a more positive approach and describe two very unique cases that I think, and some of you may disagree, show the potential for aggregation procedures and their need in situations that would be impossible to resolve effectively by individual litigation. Admittedly, I am a bit messianic about these two. The first is about football. I suspect you all know about football, but remember, what you call football is different from American football, which is closer to Rugby than your sport, which we call soccer. In the United States football is played at its highest level by very large, powerful professionals in the National Football League (NFL) wearing potentially hurtful equipment playing with an oddly shaped leather ball. The game's objective in part is, "How hard can I hit my opponent to keep him away from the ball while I try to run or throw it across a goal line?" Today, it's America's number one sport.

Sadly, it turns out, after years of speculation and studying epidemiological data about the physical condition of retired professional football players showing that a significant number of them had sustained brain damage, and many of them had experienced early deaths or committed suicide. The scientific evidence indicated that the violent body contact during the games caused repetitive concus-

---

[59] The appellate court indicated the case should not have been certified and characterized the settlement as "worthless." The lawyers' fees were denied. Another case of questionable motivation and lack of possible benefit to class members is In re Aqua Dots Prods. Liability Litigation, 654 F.3d 748 (2011).

[60] *See, e.g.,* Federal Rules 16 (case management); 23 (class actions); 26 (discovery); 41 (dismissal); 56 (summary judgment).

sions and ultimately various brain injuries. Multiple individual and aggregated actions were brought by former players and then consolidated as an MDL on behalf of over 20,000 retired NFL players. Initially, most people said the case was too weak and would be dismissed.

But it wasn't. After several years of intense and very expensive pretrial litigation carefully managed by a very talented federal judge, the parties negotiated a settlement on a class action basis that some estimates say eventually will cost the League more than two billion dollars[61]. The settlement was approved by the district judge[62] and affirmed on appeal[63]. Any retired National Football League player who develops symptoms of certain diseases in the next 65 years will be compensated and taken care of medically; the federal court will retain jurisdiction to administer the decree and make certain its terms are carried out. What each retired player will receive should he become affected with one of the covered maladies will depend on such factors as what his medical condition is, how many years he played in the NFL, and whether he played one of the positions involving significant body contact[64].

---

[61] In re Nat'l Football League Players' Concussion Injury Litig., 2015 WL 13706829 (E.D. Pa. 2015).

[62] The district judge rejected the first proposed settlement because after examining it she became concerned about whether its financial terms were sufficient to provide funding for all of the retired players. After renewed negotiation by the parties, new terms were presented that satisfied the judge.

[63] In re Nat'l Football League Players' Concussion Injury Litig., 821 F.3d 410 (3d Cir. 2016). The Supreme Court denied certiorari review on multiple occasions. See, e.g., Gilchrist v. Nat'l Football League, 137 S. Ct. 591 (2016); Armstrong v. Nat'l Football League, 137 S. Ct. 607 (2016).

[64] I suspect it will prove true in your country, as it has in mine, that almost all class actions (and MDL's) are settled. Many of them are too big or risky to litigate. Settlements in most large aggregated cases in the United States involve multiple millions of dollars – in some cases billions of dollars. See CORNERSTONE RESEARCH, SECURITIES CLASS ACTION SETTLEMENTS: 2023 REVIEW AND ANALYSIS 7 (2024), https://www.cornerstone.com/wp-content/uploads/2024/03/

As a class action, the judgment is binding on all retired players. It gives litigation peace to the NFL, it assures the consistent treatment of all class members, it provides compensation to all of the negatively affected retired players, and offers continuing supervision by a federal judge who will assure that the settlement is enforced fairly according to its terms. It would be impossible to achieve that resolution without a workable aggregation procedure. Simply impossible. To me, that is something courts should embrace.

The second case is what I think may be one of the most adventuresome example of aggregation in the post 1966 era. It is not a pleasant piece of history. Let me start by introducing someone from the audience: this is Deborah M. Sturman. For 10 years she was a distinguished French horn player with two of Europe's finest symphony orchestras. After the fall of the Berlin Wall and the reunification of Germany, she studied the East German files compiled by various of its security organizations. Then she turned to law school.

As many of you know, during World War II, particularly from '43 on, the Germans used slave labor from the concentration camps to produce military equipment under contracts with more than 30 private companies; most of them I am certain would be instantaneously recognizable by you. Slave labor was thought necessary for the war effort and was economically advantageous for the companies that used it[65]. There was a labor shortage in Germany because all eligible males were in the military and many women had essential jobs or were needed for home duties[66].

Securities-Class-Action-Settlements-2023-Review-and-Analysis.pdf (the average settlement amount in 2023 for securities class action settlements was $47.3 million dollars).

[65] Among other things, she found Gestapo documents showing the economic value of a slave laborer, including the disposition value of the body of the worker.

[66] And, by the way, I note by way of footnote, not to make you feel bad, there were a couple of Italian companies among the defendants. They were insurance companies, operating in Switzerland and Italy that had sold life policies that they never paid and property policies that also were never paid.

I have known Ms. Sturman ever since she came to New York City after law school more than twenty-five years ago to solicit interest in her idea of suing German companies to recover compensation for the work performed by the slave laborers[67]. The companies had profited from that labor without paying any wages for it[68]. Her theory was based on a simple contract notion – if someone works and performs services that are beneficial to another, that person is entitled to compensation from the recipient. She argued to a group of lawyers at a meeting I attended that despite the passage of sixty years and even though the work was performed thousands of miles from the United States, and despite the fact that the logistical reality was that the surviving slave laborers and the dependents and heirs of those who had died, were one or two generations removed from the actual slave laborers and were dispersed all over the globe, the defendants should and were legally obligated to compensate the members of a slave laborer class for the work that had been performed.

Of course the listeners confronted her with the realities that the case was incredibly risky, would be defended by some of the best American law firms, would be very expensive and protracted, would prove uneconomical even if the class could avoid a pretrial dismissal, and class counsel would have to proceed on a contingent basis. Several people in the group asked what was the value of a slave laborer's work during World War II. She replied it was between 11 and 13

---

[67] Some of Ms. Sturman's recollections are recorded in Deborah M. Sturman, *Germany's Reexamination of Its Past Through the Lens of the Holocaust Litigation, in* Holocaust Restitution, Perspectives on the Litigation and Its Legacy 215 (Michael J. Bazylor & Roger P. Alford eds., 2005). *See generally* John Authers & Richard Wolffe, The Victim's Fortune. Inside the Epic Battle over the Debts of the Holocaust (2002).

[68] In the 1990s, cases were brought against over two dozen significant German companies (Daimler, BMW, Volkswagen to name a few) in the United States District Court for New Jersey for the right to be paid for the work the laborers had performed. *See also* Arthur R. Miller, *Keynote Address: the American Class Action: From Birth to Maturity*, 19 Theoretical Inquiries in Law 12 (2014).

cents an hour. Audience members initially scoffed at those numbers because they were so low and the cases would be so costly and risky that litigation did not seem feasible. She responded with some simple arithmetic, saying: multiply 11 to 13 cents an hour by 12 hours a day, seven days a week for eight to eleven months (the average life expectancy of a slave laborer) for approximately 200,000 class members, put it at interest and compound that amount for sixty years. The resulting total she asserted would be billions of dollars of potential recovery. Billions of dollars that might help many of the survivors or their successors who were living at or below poverty level in Eastern Europe and elsewhere. I watched as the economic prospects of an aggregated class action or MDL was appreciated by the group. Obviously individual litigation was impossible; the claims had to be aggregated or left unredressed.

The matter was never litigated on its merits[69]. It was too risky for the German companies and the German government to permit litigation because it involved too many World War II participants, would create sustained adverse publicity for the companies, involved very difficult jurisdictional problems, and raised serious diplomatic issues for the United States and several other Nations. So the matter was settled after considerable negotiation for about 10 billion marks – then approximately 7.5 billion dollars[70]. Next time you visit a Ho-

---

[69] The cases arguably could have satisfied all the class action prerequisites in Rule 23 or secure MDL treatment but presented numerous procedural, statute of limitations defenses, and jurisdictional obstacles. Two federal district judges dismissed the cases before them by concluding they could not be heard in the United States. *See* United States Iwanowa v. Ford Motor Co., 67 F. Supp. 2d 424 (D.N.J. 1999); Burger-Fischer v. Degoussa AG, 65 F. Supp. 2d 248 (D.N.J. 1999). Both were appealed but never heard by the court of appeals because the matter was resolved outside of court.

[70] Eight nations resolved the matter with a letter of agreement obligating the defendants to create the fund for "remembrance" and everyone agreed to cease the class actions leaving the underlying procedure and substantive questions un-

locaust remembrance museum anywhere, there is a good chance that it was created or supported by money from that fund[71].

What do you think was the settlement amount too much or perhaps too little for the class? Opinions differ. But to me the episode illustrates the aggressiveness and creativity of American contingent fee lawyers and demonstrates the value of aggregation as a procedure that provides access to the civil justice system and the possibility of some remediation for injuries that otherwise would go unredressed.

To repeat, I believe in the vitality of the class action and some of the other aggregation devices that have been developing in the United States in recent decades[72]; in today's world, access to civil justice, which in many contexts governs the ability of people to have a grievance heard becomes a realistic possibility only through aggregation. The ideal that everyone has an individual right to an actual day in court may have been plausible when the typical dispute was between two people about an oxcart or a horse. Individual adjudication is not realistic when the dispute is between a global chemical, automobile, drug, or high-tech company and thousands of similarly situated ordinary people; nor is it effective in dealing with a mass phenomenon, such as a natural disaster or stock fraud. Neither of the disputes I have just described against the NFL or numerous powerful German companies, realistically could have been instituted let alone adjudicated in an endless series of individual actions. But critically, when the only possible day in court is representative or collective rather than actual or individual, the system must provide serious procedural mechanisms with safeguards and meaningful judicial control of all

---

resolved. Westlaw does not show any subsequent history for the district court decisions in Iwanowa or Burger-Fischer.

[71] Many of the class members did not want the money for themselves; instead they wanted their deceased relatives and what they had gone through remembered. Thus, approximately $500 million was set aside for Holocaust museums and monuments.

[72] *See* the discussion on pages 16-19, above, and accompanying footnotes.

aspects of the proceeding so that the fundamental rights of every one of the parties – both absentees and defendants – are not compromised.

I wish you all good fortune with the implementation of Italy's new class action provisions. I hope you employ them with a sense of adventure and exploit their great capacity for societal good. But be aware of the possible defects and shortcomings of the present provisions and try to improve them. Be cautioned: you may have to confront those who apparently are not very enthusiastic about giving others meaningful access to the civil justice system.

2 Class Actions and New Forms of Aggregate Litigation in the United States: A Response to Professor Arthur R. Miller

*Helen Hershkoff**

Thank you for the opportunity to return to Bocconi University after my participating in last year's discussion of Italian civil procedure reform[1]. I am honored to appear today with my esteemed senior col-

---

* Helen Hershkoff is the Herbert M. and Svetlana Wachtell Professor of Constitutional Law and Civil Liberties at New York University School of Law. She received her B.A. from Harvard College and her J.D. from Harvard Law School, and attended St. Anne's College, Oxford University, as a Marshall Scholar, earning an M.A. (Oxon.) in Modern History. She joined the NYU faculty in 1995 after an acclaimed career as a public interest lawyer at The Legal Aid Society of New York and the American Civil Liberties Union. She has received numerous awards for teaching, and her scholarship has been published in the Harvard, Stanford, Michigan, NYU, and other leading U.S. law reviews. This article is adapted from remarks she delivered at Bocconi University on May 10, 2024. She thanks Professor Cesare Cavallini for inviting her and for his gracious hospitality and intellectual companionship, together with that of Stefania Cirillo, a Post-Doctoral Research Fellow, and Professor Marcello Gaboardi, during her stay in Milan. Appreciation also goes to Aaron Kruk, Micah Musser, and Talya Nevins, students at New York University School of Law, for research assistance, to Clement Lin for library support, to Tiffany Scruggs for administrative assistance, and to Stephen Loffredo for helpful comments.

[1] On May 11, 2023, the author participated in an event, titled "The Americanization of the Italian Civil Proceedings?", at the Department of Legal Studies at Bocconi University, together with Professor Cesare Cavallini and Professor Marcello Gaboardi. Their remarks, with an introduction by Professor Marta

league Professor Arthur R. Miller[2]. I thank the Rector, Professor Marta Cartabia (who earlier in her extraordinary career was a fellow at New York University), and Professor Cesare Cavallini for the invitation to speak and for their kind introductions.

My official role today is that of Respondent to Professor Miller's illuminating and provocative Keynote Address[3]. A respondent's role conventionally requires the speaker first to praise and then to criticize the main presentation. Praise for Professor Miller, a University Professor at New York University, Commander of the British Empire, and premier civil procedure scholar, would be sincere but presumptuous; criticism would be unsporting and unwarranted. Instead, inspired – as I am sure all of you were – by Professor Miller's remarks, I will follow his suit and begin with a retrospective and somewhat autobiographical account of class actions in the United States. My story takes us back to the late 1970s in New York, more than a decade after the 1966 rule reforms that Professor Miller discussed in his Keynote Address. Fresh out of the Harvard Law School, I began my career as a litigation associate at a corporate law firm in New York, where I undertook pro bono representation in a class action involving constitutional claims against the State of New York[4]. I later left the firm to practice full-time at public

---

Cartabia, will appear in a special edition of the New York University School of Law JOURNAL OF INTERNATIONAL LAW AND POLITICS (forthcoming, 2025).

[2] Arthur R. Miller is a University Professor at New York University. *See* NYU Law Faculty, Arthur R. Miller, https://its.law.nyu.edu/facultyprofiles/index. cfm?fuseaction=profile.overview&personid=20130.

[3] Arthur R. Miller, Keynote Address, *Class Actions and New Forms of Aggregate Litigation in the United States*, Bocconi University (May 10, 2024).

[4] "Pro bono" representation in the United States refers to the provision of uncompensated legal representation by lawyers who work at for-profit law firms. *See* Deborah L. Rhode, *Pro Bono in Principle and in Practice*, 53 J. LEGAL EDUC. 413, 416 (2003) (defining pro bono service as "uncompensated"); *see also* Debra S. Katz & Lynne Bernabei, *Practicing Law in a Private Public Interest Law Firm: The Ideal Setting to Challenge the Power*, 96 W. VA. L. REV. 293 (1993/1994) (de-

interest, non-profit organizations where I again served as class action counsel in cases asserting violations of constitutional and other
rights. After recounting this history and its relation to class action
practice, I will then look forward and take a prospective approach,
offering thoughts on new forms of aggregate litigation that I see
taking shape in the United States in the shadow of Federal Rule 23[5].
These developments will take us not only to the federal courts, but
also to state courts, before arbitral panels, and to federal administrative agencies, and they involve not only litigation formally marked
as aggregative, but also single-case actions that result in nationwide
remedies on behalf of large groups of affected persons.

I emphasize at the outset that these practices are emerging in a
political and cultural context quite different from that of the period
Professor Miller described in the lead-up to the 1966 class action
amendments. As Professor Miller has emphasized, the chief goal
of the drafters of the 1966 rule was to substitute a functional definition of the class for the conceptual approach that the 1938 ver-
sion contained[6]. Their procedural goal coincided with a period of
political fervent in the United States, in which social movements,

---

scribing for-profit law firms that provide legal representation at reduced billing
rates). "Public interest, nonprofit organization" refers to law practices typically
organized as "charitable" entities exempt from federal taxation and that often
receive grants from foundations to support the practice. *Id.* at 295 (explaining the
distinction). *See generally* Helen Hershkoff & David Hollander, *Rights into Action:
Public Interest Litigation in the United States*, in MANY ROADS TO JUSTICE: THE
LAW RELATED WORK OF FORD FOUNDATION GRANTEES AROUND THE WORLD
89, 89-125 (Mary McClymont & Stephen Golub eds., 2000); Helen Hershkoff
& Aubrey McCutcheon, *Public Interest Litigation: An International Perspective*, in
id, at 283-96.

[5] Fed. R. Civ. P. 23 governs class actions in the federal courts of the United
States.

[6] *See* Arthur R. Miller, *Of Frankenstein Monsters and Shining Knights: Myths,
Reality, and the "Class Action Problem"*, 92 HARV. L. REV. 664, 669 (1979) (arguing
that the 1966 drafters "had few, if any, revolutionary notions about its work product", and instead were concerned with providing "more functional definitions of

comprised of groups previously excluded from the American polity, sought through law to make the United States more inclusive and fair. The 1966 rule drafters fully appreciated the importance of the injunctive class action to the legal struggle against racial segregation[7] and for the broader realization of egalitarian goals[8]. Moreover, they assumed that the Supreme Court of the United States, when interpreting procedural rules, would play a "democratic-promoting" role in favor of judicial access and constitutional accountability[9]. The rule drafters were not alone in this vision and aspiration. Congress and the President supported these efforts by enacting major civil rights laws that targeted racial discrimination

---

class actions", as well as codifying "the better class action practices that federal judges had developed").

[7] *See* Barak Atiram, *From* Brown *to Rule 23: The Rise and Fall of the Social Reform Class Action*, 37 Rev. Litig. 47, 54 (2018) ("The dominance of the class action device in desegregation cases came to the fore when all the legal suits, which would later be consolidated under the name of *Brown*, were submitted as class actions".); *see also* Comments, *The Class Action Device in Antisegregation Cases*, 20 U. Chi. L. Rev. 577, 577 (1953) (advocating use of the class action device to redress segregation, defined as "any policy of discriminatory treatment of a minority group").

[8] Leading up to 1966, the Court in a series of decisions, some of which took the class action form, expanded constitutional protections for members of different historically marginalized groups. *See, e.g.*, Brown v. Board of Education, 347 U.S. 483 (1954) (declaring state-mandated school segregation unconstitutional); Baker v. Carr, 396 U.S. 186 (1962) (finding malapportionment of voting districts a justiciable question under the Fourteenth Amendment); Gideon v. Wainwright, 372 U.S. 335 (1963) (requiring publicly funded counsel for indigent criminal defendants under the Sixth Amendment); Griswold v. Connecticut, 381 U.S. 479 (1965) (affirming a constitutional right to privacy and invalidating restrictions on the use of contraception); Miranda v. Arizona, 384 U.S. 436 (1966) (finding that the Fifth Amendment requires arresting officers to warn persons of various constitutional rights before interrogation).

[9] The term "democratic-promoting" is borrowed from Douglas NeJaime & Reva Siegel, *Answering the* Lochner *Objection: Substantive Due Process and the Role of Courts in a Democracy*, 96 N.Y.U. L. Rev. 1902, 1953-58 (2021).

in voting[10], public accommodations and employment[11], and housing[12], as well as laws aimed at protecting consumers[13] and the environment[14]. Admittedly, the 1966 rule drafters did not focus on the
damages class action as a mechanism for redressing mass torts and
protecting consumers from shoddy or dangerous products[15]. But
their enthusiasm for the class action to expand access to justice was
inspiring and infectious. Indeed, procedural scholars around the
world looked to U.S. courts as a model for judicial and procedural
reform[16].

Today, the United States finds itself in a very different political and
legal climate. The public shows declining trust in courts and law[17].

---

[10] *See* Voting Rights Act of 1965 (codified as amended at 52 U.S.C. §§ 10301-
10314, 10501-10508, 10701-10702).

[11] *See* Title II and Title VII of the Civil Rights Act of 1964 (codified as
amended in scattered sections of 42 U.S.C.).

[12] *See* Title VIII of the Civil Rights Act of 1968 (codified as amended at 42
U.S.C. §§ 3601–3609).

[13] *See* Fair Packaging and Labeling Act of 1966 (codified at 15 U.S.C. §§
1451-1461); Wholesome Meat Act of 1967 (codified at 21 U.S.C. ch. 12); Truth
in Lending Act of 1968 (codified at 15 U.S.C. ch. 41).

[14] *See* Clean Air Act of 1963 (codified at 42 U.S.C. ch. 85); Wilderness Act of
1964 (codified at 16 U.S.C. ch. 23); National Environmental Policy Act of 1970
(codified at 42 U.S.C. §§ 4321 *et seq.*); Clean Water Act of 1972 (codified at 33
U.S.C. §§ 1251–1387).

[15] *See* Judith Resnik, *From "Cases" to "Litigation"*, 54-3 L. & CONTEMP. PROBS.
5, 11 (1991) (contending that the 1966 drafters "did not see the class action as
responsive to the problems of mass torts"); *see also* David Marcus, *The History of
the Modern Class Action, Part II: Litigation and Legitimacy, 1981-1994*, 86 FORD-
HAM L. REV. 1785 (2018) (addressing Rule 23's history from 1981 to 1994, when
advocates used the class action to redress mass torts).

[16] *See* Helen Hershkoff, *An American's View of "The Americanization of the Italian
Civil Proceeding": Procedural Convergence, Strategic Signaling, and Democratic Process*, 57 N.Y.U. J. OF INT. L. & PUB. POL. --- (2025, forthcoming) (discussing the
influence of U.S. procedure on court reform in non-U.S. legal systems).

[17] In a 2022 Gallup poll, only 40% of U.S. adults approved of how the Supreme Court was handling its role, with 58% disapproving. *See* Jeffrey M. Jones,

The administrative state is unraveling[18]. Democracy itself seems to be on the ropes[19]. Scholars who once revered the Supreme Court for its principled commitment to the rule of law, equality, and fairness, now criticize it as being "imperial"[20] and even "oligarchic"[21]. And the class action—long associated with protecting rights and encouraging accountability—in some cases now runs counter to these earlier democratic goals. In particular, the Supreme Court has made it more difficult for workers, consumers, and historically marginalized groups to use the class action to enforce statutory and constitutional

---

Supreme Court Trust, Job Approval at Historical Lows, GALLUP (Sept. 29, 2022), https://news.gallup.com/poll/402044/supreme-court-trust-job-approval-histor-ical-lows.aspx. The disapproval and approval ratings were a historical high and low, respectively. *Id.* Indeed, legitimacy of the Supreme Court has become a hot topic within scholarly circles. *See* Ryan D. Doerfler & Samuel Moyn, *Democratizing the Supreme Court*, 109 CALIF. L. REV. 1703 (2021) ("According to the most popular scholarly frame for coming to grips with the situation, the problem with the Supreme Court is that it is suffering from a bout of institutional delegitimation").

[18] The Court has curtailed the rule making and enforcement powers of administrative agencies in ways that seriously restrict the government's ability to respond to current social and economic problems. *See, e.g.*, Loper Bright Enters. v. Raimondo, 144 S. Ct. 2244 (2024) (overruling the principle of deference to agency interpretation of regulatory law established in Chevron U.S.A., Inc. v. NRDC, 467 U.S. 837 (1984)); SEC v. Jarkesy, 144 S. Ct. 2117 (2024) (limiting the availability of administrative courts to adjudicate SEC enforcement actions). Moreover, some Justices have signaled their interest in further administrative retrenchment. *See, e.g.*, Gundy v. United States, 588 U.S. 128, 150 (2019) (Gorsuch, J., dissenting) (calling for the revival of the non-delegation doctrine).

[19] *See* Helen Hershkoff & Stephen Loffredo, *Standing for Democracy: Is Democracy a Procedural Right in Vacuo? A Democratic Perspective on Procedural Violations as a Basis for Article III Standing*, 70 BUFF. L. REV. 523, 584-610 (2022) (exploring how shifts in standing doctrine are contributing to democratic erosion).

[20] Mark A. Lemley, *The Imperial Supreme Court*, 136 HARV. L. REV. F. 97 (2022).

[21] Helen Hershkoff & Luke Norris, *The Oligarchic Courthouse: Jurisdiction, Corporate Power, and Democratic Decline*, 122 MICH. L. REV. 1 (2023).

rights[22]. Moreover, in some cases the Court has seemed determined to convert multiparty litigation into a mechanism for rights retrenchment[23], cutting back on voter protections[24], raising barriers to racial integration and racial equality[25], and eliminating the right to an abortion[26]. Looking forward, my focus thus will be not only on the technical ways in which procedure is adapting, but also on whether procedural innovation is serving—or undermining—the key goal of the Federal Rules of Civil Procedure: "the just, speedy, and inexpensive determination of every action and proceeding"[27].

------

[22] For the argument that the Supreme Court has interpreted the rules of procedure to restrict access to courts and remedies in ways that favor corporate interests at the expense of workers and consumers, *see, e.g., id.,* (discussing the deregulatory impact of the Court's procedural and jurisdictional decisions); Luke Norris, *Neoliberal Civil Procedure*, 12 U.C. IRVINE L. REV. 471 (2022) (arguing neoliberal ideology informs the Court's interpretation of the Federal Rules of Civil Procedure in a manner that restricts citizen access to civil litigation).

[23] *See* Vlad Perju, *The Second Coming of Political Liberalism: Constitutional Essentials*, 137 HARV. L. REV. 1905, 1905 (2024) ("The U.S. Supreme Court is on a crusade to revisit basic doctrines and to undo core constitutional protections"). For a discussion of the current litigation campaign to disincorporate the Bill of Rights, see Stephen J. Markman, *Toward a More Confident State Constitutionalism*, 25 FEDERALIST SOC'Y REV. 132, 140 (2024) (calling for a "dynamic era of judicial counter-reform" based on state court interpretations of state constitutions that might influence federal court interpretation of the federal Constitution).

[24] *See, e.g.,* Shelby County v. Holder, 570 U.S. 529 (2013) (striking down the § 4(b) coverage formula of the Voting Rights Act).

[25] *See, e.g.,* Students for Fair Admissions, Inc. v. President and Fellows of Harvard College, 600 U.S. 181 (2023) (striking down use of race in college admissions even to overcome historic discrimination against Black persons); Parents Involved in Community Schools v. Seattle School Dist. No. 1, 551 U.S. 701 (2007) (striking down school district plans taking race into account in assigning students to schools even to overcome historic discrimination against Black persons).

[26] *See, e.g.,* Dobbs v. Jackson Women's Health Organization, 597 U.S. 215 (2022) (overruling Roe v. Wade, 410 U.S. 113 (1973)).

[27] Fed. R. Civ. P. 1.

With this background, I begin with retrospection and autobiography.

Professor Miller's account of Federal Rule 23 began in the mid-1960s[28]. Mine begins in the late 1970s when I signed up to be a litigation associate at a large New York law firm. The firm enjoyed a well-deserved reputation for encouraging its associates to do pro bono work, but I did not expect to work on Rule 23(b)(3) lawsuits— actions that provide damages as a class wide remedy[29]. That species of class action increasingly provided large groups of consumers, shareholders, and mass tort victims with a mechanism for asserting damages claims, large and small, against private companies and corporations[30]. My law firm's clients consisted of the banks, insurance companies, and Fortune 500 companies that typically appeared as defendants in such actions; my participation as class counsel would have raised conflicts of interest, whether actual or perceived—and if not a direct conflict, at least an indirect conflict with a client's strategic interests[31]. I focused instead on Rule 23(b)

---

[28] Miller, *supra* note 3.

[29] Rule 23(b)(3) provides for class actions when "questions of law or fact common to class members predominate over any questions affecting only individual members". Fed. R. Civ. P. 23(b)(3).

[30] *See generally*, 7A CHARLES ALAN WRIGHT, ARTHUR R. MILLER & MARY KAY KANE, FEDERAL PRACTICE AND PROCEDURE: CIVIL §§ 1781.1, 1782-1783 (3d ed. 2005) (providing background on Rule 23(b)(3) and its use in suits against private companies).

[31] *See* John S. Dzienkowski, *Positional Conflicts of Interest*, 71 TEX. L. REV. 457, 461 (1993) ("A positional conflict of interest occurs when a law firm adopts a legal position for one client seeking a particular legal result that is directly contrary to the position taken on behalf of another present or former client, seeking an opposite legal result, *in a completely unrelated matter*"). "Positional conflicts" of this sort are distinct from the kinds of conflicts Rule 23(a) addresses with the goal of ensuring adequate representation of absentee class members, but they are related. *See* Fed. R. Civ. P. 23(a); WRIGHT, MILLER & KANE, *supra* note 30, at § 1768 (describing the adequacy of representation requirement for class certification under Rule 23(a)).

(2) suits against the government[32], perfect for a lawyer schooled in the hopes and ideals of the Warren Court[33]. These suits, which had come to be known as "structural reform" lawsuits[34], sought injunctive and declaratory relief, and took aim at practices affecting large numbers of similarly situated people who often were marginalized and without market or political power—and *Brown v. Board of Education* stood as the canonical example[35]. The goal of the lawsuit was not simply to overturn the pernicious regime of "separate but equal" that consigned Black children to racially isolated and unequal public schools, but also to reform racially biased institutions such as school boards that made it politically impossible for this marginalized group to secure equality under law[36]. In *Brown*, the Court declared that state-sponsored school segregation violated the Equal Protection Clause of the Fourteenth Amendment to the U.S. Constitution[37]. In a later action, the Court affirmed a forward-looking injunctive remedy, directing the district courts to implement the right to a non-segregated education and to supervise its implemen-

---

[32] *See* Maureen Carroll, Alexandra D. Lahav, Adam Zimmerman & David Marcus, *Government Class Actions After* Jennings v. Rodriguez, HARV. L. REV.: BLOG (May 8, 2018), https://harvardlawreview.org/blog/2018/05/government-class-actions-after-jennings-v-rodriguez/ (arguing that Rule 23(b)(2) was written to promote group challenges to unlawful government practices).

[33] See Thomas Geoghegan, *Warren Court Children*, NEW REPUBLIC (May 19, 1986), https://newrepublic.com/article/104659/warren-court-children.

[34] *See* Myriam E. Gilles, *Reinventing Structural Reform Litigation: Deputizing Private Citizens in the Enforcement of Civil Rights*, 100 COLUM. L. REV. 1384, 1391-92 (2000) (describing "structural reform injunctions" and their mandate that "forward-looking, affirmative steps be taken to prevent future deprivations").

[35] Brown v. Board of Education, 346 U.S. 483 (1954).

[36] Gilles, *supra* note 34, at 1391-92 (explaining how structural reform litigation came "[i]n response to findings of constitutional deprivations"); *see also* John C. Jeffries, Jr. & George A. Rutherglen, *Structural Reform Revisited*, 95 CALIF. L. REV. 1387 (2007) (arguing that structural reform litigation is most warranted when effective alternatives for the vindication of constitutional rights are absent).

[37] Brown, 346 U.S. at 495.

tation[38]. Soon counsel on behalf of other groups, including prisoners, immigrants, the mentally ill, and the developmentally disabled, likewise marginalized and excluded from constitutional protection, also filed structural reform class actions in federal court seeking to have rights declared and enforced[39].

Around 1980, I joined the litigation team of an ongoing federal class action challenging conditions at the Willowbrook State School, a public institution in New York for people who in those days— as set out in the caption of the case—were stigmatically marked as "retarded"[40]. The lawsuit had begun eight years earlier, in 1972. At the time, Willowbrook housed more than 5,000 developmentally disabled residents—almost five times its residential capacity. Senator Robert F. Kennedy called the institution a "snake pit"[41]. The lawsuit was one of a number of challenges using the class action to enforce rights on behalf of the developmentally disabled[42], and the

---

[38] Brown v. Board of Education, 349 U.S. 294 (1955).

[39] Arthur Miller, Keynote Address, *The American Class Action: From Birth to Maturity*, 19 THEORETICAL INQUIRIES 1, 14 (2018) (describing how "the class action slowly but predictably began to be employed outside the world of racial segregation and entered many other areas of discrimination" such as "gender, ethnicity, disability, age"); *see also* WRIGHT, MILLER & KANE, *supra* note 30, § 1771 ("The Advisory Committee Note to the 1966 amendment to Federal Rule of Civil Procedure 23 indicates that Rule 23(b)(2) is intended to function as an effective vehicle for the bringing of suits alleging racial discrimination. Thus, perhaps not surprisingly, many courts embraced this notion and encouraged the use of the class action not only in cases concerning racial discrimination but also in actions involving a variety of civil rights and liberties").

[40] *See* N.Y. State Ass'n for Retarded Children v. Carey, 393 F. Supp. 715, 716-17 (E.D.N.Y. 1975) (hereinafter "*Carey I*"); *see also* The Bryant Park Project, *Remembering an Infamous New York Institution*, NAT'L PUB. RADIO (March 7, 2008), https://www.npr.org/2008/03/07/87975196/remembering-an-infamous-new-york-institution.

[41] The Bryant Park Project, *supra* note 40.

[42] *See, e.g.*, Welsch v. Likins, 373 F. Supp. 487 (D. Minn. 1974) (class action seeking declaratory and injunctive relief under the Civil Rights Act regarding treatment and conditions in children's mental hospitals and alternatives to

Willowbrook case became an important model for later challenges of this kind[43].

The lawyer-team consisted of not-for-profit counsel from The Legal Aid Society and the New York Civil Liberties Union, assisted by pro bono counsel[44]. Following extensive discovery and a trial, the district court in 1975 had entered a consent decree that set standards for running the institution—which meant providing at a minimum food, water, and medicine, as well as appropriate education and care[45]. The decree also called for the relocation of residents into community based, supportive housing to carry out the due process requirement that persons be detained in the least restrictive setting possible[46]. Moreover, the decree established a governance structure comprised of experts, doctors, parents, and

---

placement in those institutions), *aff'd*, 550 F.2d 1122 (8th Cir. 1977); Gary W. v. Louisiana, 437 F. Supp. 1209 (E.D. La. 1976); Horacek v. Exon, 357 F. Supp. 71 (D. Neb. 1973) (class action seeking injunctive relief against mistreatment of children at state home for developmentally disabled under the Eighth Amendment); Wyatt v. Stickney, 344 F. Supp. 387 (M.D. Ala. 1972) (class action alleging that Alabama state school designed to habilitate the mentally disabled was being operated in a constitutionally impermissible fashion), *aff'd in part, rev'd in part and remanded sub nom.* Wyatt v. Aderholt, 503 F.2d 1395 (5th Cir. 1974).

[43] *50 Years After a Landmark Lawsuit, How Does NY Treat People with Developmental Disabilities?*, N.Y. C.L. Union (Oct. 13, 2022), https://www.nyclu.org/commentary/50-years-after-landmark-lawsuit-how-does-ny-treat-people-developmental-disabilities ("The landmark legal settlement [in *Carey* I] established a standard of care for people with developmental and intellectual disabilities and was in the vanguard of the civil rights movement for people with disabilities") [hereinafter "*50 Years After*"].

[44] *See generally* David J. Rothman & Sheila M. Rothman, The Willowbrook Wars: Bringing the Mentally Disabled into the Community (1984).

[45] *Carey I*, 393 F. Supp. at 716-17.

[46] *See* N.Y. State Ass'n for Retarded Children v. Carey, 706 F.2d 956, 959 (2d Cir. 1983).

high-functioning residents to monitor conditions, assess progress, and resolve disputes[47].

What the decree did not do was ask the federal court to "command-and-control" the institution—a frequent but unfounded criticism of structural reform litigation[48]. Rather, the decree asked the court to hold government officials accountable for actions that caused indisputable harm, both mental and physical, to persons placed in the care of the state[49]. The class action provided the procedural mechanism for declaring rights and enforcing remedies among a large group of similarly affected persons, and the relief fell comfortably within the scope of the federal judicial power. However, without the class action mechanism, securing these protections would have been impracticable if not impossible.

Scholars view the Willowbrook decree as a highly successful example of using the injunctive class action to enforce rights against government actors and to encourage political support for rights of a politically marginalized group[50]. The case highlighted and re-

---

[47] *Carey I*, 393 F. Supp. at 717 ("[The consent decree] further provides for the appointment of a Review Panel to monitor implementation of the judgment and to perform other functions, as well as a Professional Advisory Board and a Consumer Advisory Board for Willowbrook").

[48] *See* Charles F. Sabel & William H. Simon, *Destabilization Rights: How Public Law Litigation Succeeds*, 117 HARV. L. REV. 1015, 1021-22 (2004) (explaining the critique of "command-and-control" decrees).

[49] *See Carey I*, 393 F. Supp. at 717.

[50] *See 50 Years After, supra* note 43; The Bryant Park Project, *supra* note 40. *See The Closing of Willowbrook*, DISABILITY JUSTICE (2022), https://disabilityjustice. org/the-closing-of-willowbrook/. *See also* Sabel & Simon, *supra* note 48, at 1080 ("In the Willowbrook case, the shift from institutional to community placement was accompanied by the emergence of nonprofit groups that wanted to run the new facilities and of real estate interests that wanted to profit from their development. Both groups gave important support to the plaintiffs' efforts, leading close observers of these events to conclude that 'the process of opening group homes, like that of contracting with the voluntary agencies, created a constituency for deinstitutionalization'").

dressed inhumane conditions; it established a remedial structure that reformed governance within the institution; and it motivated legislative action[51]. Eventually, New York closed the institution and established alternative residential facilities for persons in need of support and supervision[52]. These developments, which relied upon judicial intervention, were fortified by disability rights activism, and proved to be transformative even if incomplete and at times undermined or subverted in practice[53]. A rich scholarly literature has documented the critical role that class action litigation played in improving conditions in other institutions such as state and federal prisons[54]. Success did not mean that court-ordered relief could or did solve all of the problems—but the class action made a critical difference in the lives of the affected populations.

Indeed, the very success of the Rule 23(b)(2) lawsuit on behalf of otherwise politically powerless groups made it vulnerable as a target of backlash and criticism—and eventually it fell victim to doctrinal retrenchment. I emphasize that during this period Rule 23 did not go through formal amendment. The text of the rule did not change (changes came later). What did change was the composition of the Supreme Court of the United States, as a series of judicial vacancies created space for Presidential appointments, beginning with the Nixon Administration, that shifted the interpretive valence and normative commitments of the Justices[55]. In particular, with the shift from

---

[51] *See, e.g.,* Education for All Handicapped Children Act of 1975 (codified as amended in scattered sections of 20 U.S.C.).

[52] *The Closing of Willowbrook, supra* note 50; The Bryant Park Project, *supra* note 40.

[53] *See generally* Samuel R. Bagenstos, *The Past and Future of Deinstitutionalization Litigation*, 34 CARDOZO L. REV. 1 (2012).

[54] *See, e.g.,* MALCOLM M. FEELEY & EDWARD L. RUBIN, JUDICIAL POLICY MAKING AND THE MODERN STATE: HOW THE COURTS REFORMED AMERICA'S PRISONS (1998).

[55] *See* Robert M. Cover, *Nomos and Narrative*, 97 HARV. L. REV. 4, 58 (1983) (referring to "[t]he extraordinary capacity of small shifts in membership of the

the Warren Court to the Burger Court and then to the Rehnquist Court, the class action underwent contraction as a mechanism for enforcing rights to equality and due process[56].

In 1979, Professor Owen Fiss of the Yale Law School published *The Forms of Justice*, a major account of structural reform litigation, and he warned that the Burger Court was mounting a "counterassault" on the practice—indeed, he saw the decisions as trending toward a "counter-revolution" in the use of the Rule 23 class action[57]. He argued strenuously for the importance of the injunctive civil rights action as a democratic procedure needed to secure the rights of those who could not count on ordinary majoritarian politics to respect their rights or even guarantee their safety[58]. Yet the counterassault continued, as an increasingly conservative majority of Supreme Court justices further constrained rights enforcement with newly minted notions of federalism[59], sovereign im-

---

Supreme Court to transform not only the decisional law of that Court, but also the strategic significance of the entire federal judiciary"). The shifts in appointment to the Supreme Court in the period 1970 to 1988 were not "small." Rather, Republican presidents appointed seven justices to the Supreme Court, including Justices William Rehnquist, Sandra Day O'Connor, and Antonin Scalia, each with a conception of the role of the Article III courts that differed significantly from that of the Warren Court. *See Justices 1789 to Present*, Sup. Ct. of the U.S., https://www.supremecourt.gov/about/members_text.aspx.

[56] *See* Edward A. Purcell, Jr., *The Class Action Fairness Act in Perspective: The Old and the New in Federal Jurisdictional Reform*, 156 U. Pa. L. Rev. 1823, 1867-72 (2008) (describing the Burger and Rehnquist Courts' belief that class actions did not "belong" in federal courts, in contrast with the Warren Court's treatment); *see also* Abram Chayes, *The Supreme Court, 1981 Foreword: Public Law Litigation and the Burger Court*, 96 Harv. L. Rev. 4, 28 (1982) (arguing that the Court in a series of decisions restricted the "operation of the class action as a device for the enforcement of statutory and constitutional policies").

[57] Owen M. Fiss, *Foreword: The Forms of Justice*, 93 Harv. L. Rev. 1, 5 (1979).

[58] *Id.* at 5.

[59] *See, e.g.*, Rizzo v. Goode, 423 U.S. 362, 379 (1976) (holding that "appropriate consideration must be given to principles of federalism in determining the availability and scope of equitable relief" in federal courts).

munity[60], remedies[61], and judicial incapacity[62], blunting the utility of injunctive class actions as a tool for holding government accountable. In particular, Rule 23 became the focal point for criticisms of federal judicial "activism"[63]. What could sound like dry legal discourse about technical rules of civil procedure masked the stakes of the political debate about class action litigation: the federal courts' very commitment to "Equal Justice under Law," the lofty words inscribed on the building that houses the Supreme Court[64].

In this context, Justice William J. Brennan, Jr. weighed in from a different direction, and delivered a series of lectures, first at the Harvard Law School[65] and then at New York University Law School[66], urging state courts to step into the remedial breach created by the

---

[60] *See, e.g.*, Seminole Tribe of Florida v. Florida, 517 U.S. 44, 54 (1996) (holding that the Eleventh Amendment presupposes "each State is a sovereign entity in our federal system" and that it "is inherent in the nature of sovereignty not to be amenable to the suit of an individual without its consent").

[61] *See, e.g.*, Grupo Mexicano de Desarrollo S.A. v. All. Bond Fund, Inc., 527 U.S. 308, 332 (1999) ("[T]he equitable powers conferred by the Judiciary Act of 1789 did not include the power to create remedies previously unknown to equity jurisprudence").

[62] *See, e.g.*, Allen v. Wright, 468 U.S. 737, 750-51 (1984) (limiting the federal judicial power to "cases or controversies" where the litigant has "standing").

[63] *See* Francisco Valdes, *Procedure, Policy and Power: Class Actions and Social Justice in Historical and Comparative Perspective*, 24 Ga. St. U. L. Rev. 627 (2012) (discussing the political and cultural stakes of backlash against judicial "activism").

[64] *See* Helen Hershkoff & Judith Resnik, *Constraining and Licensing Arbitrariness: The Stakes in Debates about Substantive-Procedural Due Process*, 76 SMU L. Rev. 613, 624 (2024) ("Although that phrase is not found in the text of the Constitution, these words have been reprinted on the Court's brochures and appear hundreds of times in lower court opinions").

[65] William J. Brennan, Jr., *State Constitutions and the Protection of Individual Rights*, 90 Harv. L. Rev. 489, 491 (1977).

[66] William J. Brennan, Jr., *The Bill of Rights and the States: The Revival of State Constitutions as Guardians of Individual Rights*, 61 N.Y.U. L. Rev. 535 (1986); *see also* Helen Hershkoff, *Seventy-Fifth Anniversary Retrospective: Most Influential*

Supreme Court's retrenchment from the text and aspirations of the Fourteenth Amendment[67]. Around this time, I left the law firm and joined The Legal Aid Society in its Civil Appeals and Law Reform Unit, and transitioned later to the American Civil Liberties Union. At each, my practice was that of a civil rights and civil liberties lawyer using the injunctive class action. Those lawsuits, together with activism outside the courts, provided a lever to reform institutional conditions whether in public schools, hospitals for the mentally ill, or housing projects for the poor. However, my preferred venue no longer was the federal courts but instead state courts throughout the United States[68]. Indeed, in some of these states, it was possible to pursue a hybrid form of class action that combined injunctive relief and damages for class members who alleged a violation of constitutional rights[69].

This advocacy strategy—and Justice Brennan's admonition—accorded with the federated system that structures American governance. The federal Constitution establishes the federal court system in the United States; it assumes the existence of the states and each state has a judiciary that is separate from that of the federal courts[70]. State court judgments that raise a federal issue are subject to discre-

––––––––––

Articles, 75 N.Y.U. L. REV. 1517, 1554 (2000) (commenting on *The Bill of Rights and the States*).

[67] FRANK I. MICHELMAN, BRENNAN AND DEMOCRACY 138 (1999) ("[T]o praise Justice Brennan as a visionary, a prophet, would be to trivialize his contribution to American constitutional history. His status is altogether different. He was a framer").

[68] *See* Helen Hershkoff, *Introductory Remarks: The Promise and Limits of State Constitutions*, 99 N.Y.U. L. REV.— (2024, forthcoming) (describing shifts in forum choice from federal to state court in response to the changing composition and ideological tilt of the Supreme Court of the United States).

[69] *See, e.g.*, Ihler v. Chisholm, 259 Mont. 240 (1993) (seeking both injunctive and monetary relief for alleged civil rights violations of hospital patients). *See generally* WRIGHT, MILLER & KANE, *supra* note 30, at § 1784.1 (describing so-called federal "hybrid class actions").

[70] For a classic discussion of the relation between state courts and federal courts, and of differences "between two coordinate systems of courts", see Henry

tionary review by the Supreme Court of the United States[71]. State court procedures must comply with federal due process[72], but they are not required to conform to the Federal Rules of Civil Procedure[73]. Although the federal Constitution authorizes Congress to confer jurisdiction on the federal courts to decide state law disputes in specified circumstances[74], state law disputes are otherwise matters for state courts to decide consistent with the Supremacy Clause, and Article III of the federal Constitution generally does not limit state judicial power[75]. However, every state must respect due process and equal protection, and some state constitutions include rights that have no federal analogue[76].

M. Hart, Jr., *The Relation between State and Federal Law*, 54 COLUM. L. REV. 489, 505 (1954).

[71] *See* Martin v. Hunter's Lessee, 14 U.S. (1 Wheat.) 304 (1816) (establishing Supreme Court review of final state court judgments implicating questions of federal law).

[72] *See* Hershkoff & Resnik, *supra* note 64, at 629 (discussing as an example the application of federal due process to state court rules providing notice to litigants).

[73] For discussions of state adoption of federal procedural rules, see, for example, John B. Oakley, *A Fresh Look at the Federal Rules in State Courts*, 3 NEV. L.J. 354 (2003); Carl Tobias, *The Past and Future of the Federal Rules in State Courts*, 3 NEV. L.J. 400 (2003); John B. Oakley & Arthur F. Coon, *The Federal Rules in State Courts: A Survey of State Court Systems of Civil Procedure*, 61 WASH. L. REV. 1367 (1986); *see also* Miyoko T. Petit-Toledo, *The Politics of Proportionality in State Civil Rulemaking*, 101 DENV. L. REV. 641 (2024) (discussing, in the context of rules governing discovery, the influence of federal procedure on state procedure).

[74] *See* U.S. Const. art. III, § 2.

[75] *See* Michael E. Solimine, *Supreme Court Monitoring of State Courts in the Twenty-First Century*, 35 IND. L. REV. 335 (2002) (discussing the constitutional scope of Supreme Court review of state court judgments and shifts in the doctrine); Helen Hershkoff, *State Courts and the "Passive Virtues,"* 114 HARV. L. REV. 1833, 1836 (2001) (explaining that state courts "are not bound by Article III").

[76] *See* Goodwin Liu, *State Courts and Constitutional Structure*, 128 YALE L.J. 1304, 1314 (2019) (discussing state constitutions "as an antidote for misguided

My work at The Legal Aid Society coincided with the Reagan Administration, which had the goal of privatizing public services and shrinking government[77]. During this time, New York was experiencing a great boom in investment banking and, with it, gentrification; over time, the City suffered a dramatic loss of housing for poor people and lower income workers[78]. A housing crisis developed that over the decades has only gotten worse[79]. The federal Constitution does not guarantee any positive rights—whether to pub-

---

decisions of the U.S. Supreme Court", and as "key parts of the dynamic process by which constitutional doctrine develops over time") (book review). For a discussion of state constitutional rights to government assistance that lack any federal analogue, see Helen Hershkoff, *Positive Rights and State Constitutions: The Limits of Federal Rationality Review*, 112 Harv. L. Rev. 1131 (1999).

[77] *See* Steven G. Calabresi, *The President, the Supreme Court, and the Constitution: A Brief Positive Account of the Role of Government Lawyers in the Development of Constitutional Law*, 61-1 L. & Contemp. Probs. 61, 70 (1998) (discussing President Reagan's "long-stated goal of shrinking the size of government"); Susan Rose-Ackerman, *Defending the State: A Skeptical Look at "Regulatory Reform" in the Eighties*, 61 U. Colo. L. Rev. 517, 519 (1990) (stating that the Reagan Administration's goals were "deregulation, decentralization, and privatization").

[78] *See* Sarena Malsin, *Unveiling the "Trojan Horses" of Gentrification: Studies of Legal Strategies to Combat Environmental Gentrification in Washington, DC and New York, N.Y.*, 38 Pace Envtl. L. Rev. 147, 151 (2020) (detailing history of gentrification in Brooklyn and Manhattan, N.Y.C.). By 2016, over one third of low-income households lived in neighborhoods at risk of or already experiencing displacement and gentrification pressures, comprising 24% of the New York metropolitan area. *See* Urban Displacement Project, *Mapping Displacement and Gentrification in the New York Metropolitan Area* (2021), https://www.urbandisplacement.org/maps/new-york-gentrification-and-displacement/. *See also* Kacie L. Dragan, Ingrid Gould Ellen & Sherry A. Glied, *Gentrification and The Health of Low-Income Children In New York City*, 38-9 Health Affairs 1425 (Sept. 2019) (summarizing empirical data on gentrification in New York and its effects on low-income families and children).

[79] *See* Mark Peters, *Homelessness: A Historical Perspective on Modern Legislation*, 88 Mich. L. Rev. 1209 (1990) (giving an overview of the history of homelessness in New York City).

lic schooling, public health, or public shelter[80]. But the New York Constitution has a provision, dating to the New Deal, that speaks to the government's power and duty to provide aid and assistance to the needy[81]. Lawyers at The Legal Aid Society and other public interest groups set out to enforce that provision on behalf of people who were priced out of market-based housing and were living on the streets[82]. Heeding Justice Brennan's clarion call, poor people's advocates looked to the New York courts to enforce state constitutional duties and to help solve a problem that had evaded legislative concern.

So far, so good. We had a theory and law to support it. Nevertheless, the litigation strategy faced a procedural barrier: New York's class action rule. New York adopted its first class action statute in 1849 as an amendment to the highly influential Field Code[83]. The statute drew from Chancery Court practice dating back to the seventeenth century and Justice Story's early nineteenth-century writing on equity[84]. Like the Field Code itself, the New York class action rule became a model for other states[85]. The rule read: "[a]nd when the question is one of a common or general interest of many persons, or when the parties are very numerous and it may be impracticable to

---

[80] *See* Hershkoff, *supra* note 76, at 1132-35 (detailing the Supreme Court's repeated refusal to infer positive rights from the text of the federal Constitution).

[81] N.Y. Const. art. XVII, § 1 ("The aid, care and support of the needy are public concerns and shall be provided by the state and by such of its subdivisions, and in such manner and by such means, as the legislature may from time to time determine").

[82] *See* Michael Bobelian, *The Contentious History Behind New York City's Right to Shelter*, STATE COURT REPORT (Oct. 25, 2023), https://statecourtreport.org/our-work/analysis-opinion/contentious-history-behind-new-york-citys-right-shelter.

[83] Richard J. Schager, Jr., *What Will It Take to Reform New York's Class Action Procedures?*, 94-1 N.Y. ST. BAR J. 41, 41 (2021).

[84] *Id.*

[85] *Id.*

bring them all before the Court, one or more may sue or defend for the benefit of the whole"[86].

Today is not the occasion to parse all of the problems that the New York rule presented to using the class action as a vehicle for group redress. At least one scholar has argued that "[t]he provision may well qualify as one of the worst in the Code"[87]. Nevertheless, the rule persisted and seriously impeded class action practice. Moreover, New York courts compounded the problem by reading a privity requirement into the rule's use of the term "common"—a court would certify a class only if a jural relation existed among the parties[88]. Indeed, this very limitation had found its way into the 1938 federal class action rule[89].

In 1952, the New York Judicial Council proposed to eliminate the requirement of privity from the state's class action rule[90]; ten years later, in 1962, New York enacted that proposal, to become effective in 1963[91]. Then something curious happened. In 1962—the very year of the proposal's enactment—the legislature reversed field and decided to restore the Field Code restriction[92]. The proposal inspired the 1966 federal amendments that Professor Miller discussed in his Keynote Address[93]. However, it provided no help to those seeking to certify classes in the 1980s in New York courts under the antiquated Field Code rule.

---

[86] 1849 N.Y. Session Laws, ch. 438, § 119.

[87] Adolf Homburger, *State Class Actions and the Federal Rule*, 71 Colum. L. Rev. 609, 613 (1971).

[88] *Id.* at 615-16.

[89] *Id.* at 626-27.

[90] New York State Judicial Council, 18th Annual Report Of The Judicial Council Of The State Of New York 80, 223 (1952); *see also* Homburger, *supra* note 87, at 631.

[91] Homburger, *supra* note 87, at 631.

[92] *Id.*

[93] *Id.* ("Subdivision (a) of rule 23, as amended, is substantially identical to the New York proposal of 1962").

To make matters worse, New York courts placed other glosses on the class action rule that further limited its utility. In particular, the state courts imported a common law rule—unique to the state—that disfavored class actions against the government[94]. Of a piece with that policy, the state's highest court took the view that class certification was not superior to other methods of suit against the government, and so unnecessary, because the government could be expected to follow the law and future litigants would be "adequately protected under the principles of stare decisis"[95]. Exacerbating the difficulty faced by civil rights plaintiffs, the state procedural code entitled the government to an automatic stay of enforcement of an adverse judgment or order pending appeal[96]. Italian proceduralists know too well the problems that result from stays and appeals[97]. New York has not yet amended its class action rule, and it has not yet eliminated the state's automatic stay[98]. Since 2016, the New York Office of Court Administration has urged the

---

[94] Schager, *supra* note 83.

[95] Martin v. Lavine, 39 N.Y.2d 72, 75 (1976); *see also* Daan Braverman, *Class Certification in State Court Welfare Litigation: A Request for Procedural Justice*, 28 BUFF. L. REV. 57 (1979).

[96] N.Y. CPLR §5519(a)(1) (McKinney); *see* Jack F. Pace III, *Automatic Stays and Governmental Operations: How New York State Protects the Government from the Poor*, 24 FORDHAM URB. L.J. 137 (1996).

[97] *See* Helen Hershkoff & Stephen Loffredo, *Legal Culture, Optimal Delay, and Social Commitments: A Tribute to Vincenzo Varano*, in PROCESSO E CULTURA GIURIDICA, PROCEDURE AND LEGAL CULTURE: SCRITTI PER GLI 80 ANNI DI VINCENZO VARANO 295, 295-313 (Vittoria Barsotti & Alessandro Simoni eds., 2020) (discussing delay in the Italian court system).

[98] As of this writing, proposed amendments to New York's class action laws have been introduced in both the New York State Senate and Assembly. *See Report in support of legislation to reform and modernize the administration of class actions in New York's courts*, State Courts of Superior Jurisdiction Comm., Council on Jud. Admin. and Litig. Comm. (Mar. 14, 2024), http://www2.nycbar.org/pdf/report/uploads/20072985-ClassActionsProposedAmendsArt9CPLRJudicia-lAdminLitigationStateCourtsReportFINAL11515.pdf.

Legislature to amend the class action rule; a 2022 article published in the New York Bar Journal stated the obvious—that "modernizing the administration of class actions by the New York courts is long overdue"[99].

Much more could be said about class action litigation in New York during the 1980s—remarkably, notwithstanding the barrier posed by New York's class action rule to aggregate litigation, I can point to court victories that significantly benefited the state's poor[100]. Moreover, other states had class action rules on a par with the federal, and its availability provided an efficient mechanism for declaring and enforcing rights for large groups of persons deprived of their statutory entitlements or constitutional rights[101]. Indeed, many commentators would argue that the class action is a critical means of providing access to justice, especially in a constitutional regime such as that in the United States, that does not guarantee a right to counsel in civil actions and provides insufficient funding for legal aid—government funding supports the provision of only one lawyer for every 6,000 poor people in need of legal representation[102]. Worsening the situation, in 1996, Congress barred any advocacy group that received funding from the federal Legal Services Corporation from filing class action lawsuits, even if private funding support-

---

[99] Schager, *supra* note 83.

[100] See Appendix of Cases included in Helen Hershkoff, *Statement of Helen Hershkoff in Opposition to a Constitutional Convention*, Submitted to the Association of the Bar of the City of New York (March 22, 2017); *see also* Helen Hershkoff & Stephen Loffredo, *State Courts and Constitutional Socio-Economic Rights: Exploring the Underutilization Thesis*, 115 PENN ST. L. REV. 923 (2011).

[101] *See, e.g.*, Mathew Diller, *Poverty Lawyering in the Golden Age*, 93 MICH. L. REV. 1401 (1995).

[102] *See* Helen Hershkoff & Stephen Loffredo, GETTING BY: ECONOMIC RIGHTS AND LEGAL PROTECTIONS FOR PEOPLE WITH LOW INCOME 785 (2020) (citing statistics).

ed the specific lawsuits[103]. The restrictions could not reasonably be justified on efficiency grounds[104]. Instead, the restrictions, still in effect, serve to limit equal court access for politically marginalized persons, including those in poverty, incarcerated, and of vulnerable immigration status[105].

With this background, let me turn from the retrospective to the prospective, and discuss some of the emergent trends in aggregate litigation that I see developing in the shadow of Federal Rule 23— not only in the federal courts, but also in state courts, administrative agencies, and arbitral proceedings. To preview, some of these approaches build on the regulatory goals of the "(b)(2)" injunctive class action. Some of the approaches build on the compensatory goals of the "(b)(3)" damages action. All of these new forms of aggregation aim to deter and either substitute for or complement public enforcement mechanisms. Some of the emergent mechanisms combine the private with the public, enabling individual initiative subject to government oversight. Moreover, recognizing the importance of community engagement and citizen activism, some of these new ag-

---

[103] *See* Henry Rose, *Class Actions and the Poor*, 6 PIERCE L. REV. 55, 58 (2007) (discussing efforts during the Reagan Administration to defund the Legal Services Corporation and so to end funding for civil legal representation for the poor, and the adoption of class-action restrictions on LSC-recipients). For a list of restrictions, see *Statutory Restrictions on LSC-Funded Programs*, LEGAL SERVS. CORP., https://www.lsc.gov/our-impact/publications/other-publications-and-reports/statutory-restrictions-lsc-funded-programs.

[104] *See* Rebekah Diller & Emily Savner, *Restoring Legal Aid for the Poor: A Call to End Draconian and Wasteful Restrictions*, 36 FORDHAM URB. L.J. 687, 692 (2009) (locating the restriction in the Reagan Administration's hostility to providing funding for counsel for the poor).

[105] *See* DEBORAH L. RHODE, ACCESS TO JUSTICE 104 (2004) (noting that the "current legal aid structure denies assistance to the politically unpopular groups who are least able to do without it and blocks the strategies most likely to address the root causes of economic deprivation"); Diller & Savner, *supra* note 104, at 688 (noting restrictions placed on LSC-recipients corresponding to the above-mentioned groups).

gregative practices seek to empower group members, and especially workers and consumers.

Again, it is important to view these procedural developments in a political and cultural context that is quite different from the period described by Professor Miller in his discussion of the 1966 amendments to Federal Rule 23. Significantly, a conservative legal movement is now firmly entrenched in the United States. It has moved beyond seeking merely to weaken enforcement of civil rights and market regulation[106]. I would argue that the movement's overriding substantive goal is to expand corporate power, enhance the role of religion in the public sphere, deregulate the use of guns, and otherwise disincorporate the Bill of Rights[107]. This robust agenda is poised to leverage the class action and new forms of aggregate litigation in ways that potentially could undo the civil rights and civil liberties advances of the last half of the twentieth century[108].

So, what are some of these new forms of aggregation?

Consider, first, aggregate trends among state officials and state courts. State courts typically receive less attention than federal courts, but they are the real workhorses of the U.S. judicial system. Between 2012 and 2022, an average of 98.5 percent of U.S. court cases were filed in state courts, and only 1.5 percent were filed in

---

[106] *See, e.g.*, Stephen B. Burbank & Sean Farhang, *Rights and Retrenchment in the Trump Era*, 87 Fordham L. Rev. 37, 40 (2018) ("The counterrevolution's strategy has been to leave substantive rights in place while retrenching the infrastructure for their private enforcement").

[107] *See, e.g.*, Erwin Chemerinsky, *Equal Justice Under Law?*, 72 Am. U. L. Rev. 1449 (2023) (reporting that with the Trump Administration's appointment of three Justices to the Supreme Court, "the Roberts Court has ... moved remarkably fast and remarkably far in advancing the conservative agenda").

[108] *See, e.g.*, Myriam E. Gilles, *An Autopsy of the Structural Reform Injunction: Oops . . . It's Still Moving!*, 58 U. Miami L. Rev. 143, 146-47 (2003) (concluding "that a conservative-led effort to engage in structural reform litigation might be under way right now, epitomized by lawsuits seeking judicial decrees governing the admissions criteria of state-run educational institutions").

federal court; that's a difference of between 100 million cases filed each year in state court and 400,000 in federal trial courts[109]. Here I see three major trends in state courts: suits by Attorneys General on behalf of the residents of the state on a theory of *parens patriae* and sovereign standing; the delegation of state authority to individuals to enforce sovereign rights on the model of the federal relator statute; and the delegation of enforcement authority to individuals without any showing of injury. I also will discuss suits filed by states in federal court challenging federal policies[110].

One significant trend is the uptick in lawsuits brought by state Attorneys General that seek relief for large numbers of affected persons. In one category of cases, the state files its suit in its *parens patriae* capacity asserting a quasi-sovereign interest on behalf of state citizens; the complaint challenges wrongdoing by a private company or corporations. State-initiated lawsuits against tobacco companies for misrepresenting the health dangers of cigarette smoking are an early example of this trend[111]. The lawsuits typically invoke state law and

---

[109] Quality Judges Initiative, *FAQs: Judges in the United States*, INST. FOR THE ADVANCEMENT OF THE AM. LEGAL SYS. (June 12, 2014), https://iaals.du.edu/sites/default/files/documents/publications/judge_faq.pdf.

[110] Democratic attorneys general sued the federal government more times in the four years of the Trump Administration than they had in the previous 16. *State attorneys-general are shaping national policy*, ECONOMIST (Feb. 8, 2024), https://www.economist.com/united-states/2024/02/08/state-attorneys-general-are-shaping-national-policy. Likewise, Republican state attorneys general brought no fewer than 46 lawsuits against the Obama Administration. *See* Note, *An Abdication Approach to State Standing*, 132 HARV. L. REV. 1301, 1301 (2019) [hereinafter, *Abdication*]. Moreover, states have invested in establishing and supporting state solicitor general offices, with more than 43 states and territories now having such offices. H.W. Perry Jr., *The Elitification of the U.S. Supreme Court and Appellate Lawyering*, 72 S.C.L. REV. 245, 269 (2020).

[111] *See* Richard P. Ieyoub & Theodore Eisenberg, *State Attorney General Actions, the Tobacco Litigation, and the Doctrine of Parens Patriae*, 74 TUL. L. REV. 1859 (2000).

seek both injunctive and monetary relief[112]. Procedurally, these suits sidestep the Court's narrowed approach to Rule 23, especially with respect to the showing of commonality[113]. At the same time, they raise concerns given their preclusive effects on unrepresented parties whose rights to damages or other relief will terminate without any of the procedural protections afforded absentee class members[114]. Nevertheless, the importance of these lawsuits should not be overlooked; *parens patriae* suits today are challenging some of the most pressing problems of contemporary life, including actions against fossil fuel companies for contributing to climate change[115].

State Attorney General suits are not limited to those against private parties. Rather, state Attorneys General, sometimes in a *parens patriae* capacity, but sometimes in a sovereign capacity, also now sue agencies or officers of the federal government. States invariably file these suits in federal court and assert federal claims[116]; they seek

---

[112] *Id.* at 1863-64 (describing *parens patriae* suits, how they vindicate the public interest, and how they can seek damages). *See also* Margaret H. Lemos, *Aggregate Litigation Goes Public: Representative Suits by State Attorneys General*, 126 HARV. L. REV. 486, 488 (2012) ("Although many public suits seek injunctive relief and other remedies that are unavoidably aggregate, others seek damages or restitution for identifiable individuals who have been injured by unlawful conduct").

[113] *See* Anthony J. Sebok, *Pretext, Transparency and Motive in Mass Restitution Litigation*, 57 VAND. L. REV. 2177, 2190 (2004) (discussing states' procedural advantages in multistate tobacco litigation and noting that "[c]oncerns over common issues of fact, which doomed earlier class actions to fail the predominance and superiority tests of federal and state class action statutes, would be finessed").

[114] Lemos, *supra* note 112, at 532-48 (demonstrating the unique issues of *parens patriae* preclusion in terms of due process and proposing some solutions to those issues).

[115] *See* Ieyoub & Eisenberg, *supra* note 111, at 1869-70 (collecting *parens patriae* cases for various environmental interests); Bradford Mank, *Standing and Future Generations: Does* Massachusetts v. EPA *Open Standing for Generations to Come?*, 34 COLUM. J. ENTL.L.1 (2009) (discussing *parens patriae* in climate change litigation).

[116] *See Abdication*, *supra* note 110, at 1306-07 (describing the rise of *parens patriae* actions against the federal government by state attorneys general).

to reorient public policy by challenging existing rules and regulations and are loosely analogous to civil rights injunctive suits. Until recently, it was assumed that a state could not assert *parens patriae* standing against the federal government[117], but in 2007, the Supreme Court of the United States permitted Massachusetts, together with eleven other states and several cities, to sue the federal Environmental Protection Agency to compel regulation of emissions of carbon dioxide and other greenhouse gases[118]. Since then, there has been an extraordinary surge in state suits against the federal government with filings often following partisan political lines[119]. In less than a year, Republican Attorneys General filed more than a dozen lawsuits against the Biden Administration on such issues as vaccine mandates during the COVID-19 pandemic, immigration enforcement priorities, and the moratorium on oil and natural gas leases[120]. In April 2024, in multiple separate lawsuits, nine so-called Red states (meaning, the Republican Party dominates elected office), sued to enjoin the Biden Administration's education regulations on sexual harassment and trans rights[121].

The second trend of aggregate actions among the states involves the delegation of state enforcement authority to private parties who

---

[117] *See* Commonwealth of Massachusetts v. Mellon, 262 U.S. 447, 485 (1923) (explaining that although a state may sue "for the protection of its citizens . . . it is no part of its duty or power to enforce their rights in respect of their relations with the federal government).

[118] Massachusetts v. EPA, 549 U.S. 497 (2007).

[119] *See* William Baude & Samuel L. Bray, *Proper Parties, Proper Relief*, 137 HARV. L. REV. 153, 164 (2022) (criticizing the decision and reporting that in its wake "the number of lawsuits brought by state attorneys general challenging actions by the federal government skyrocketed" along partisan lines).

[120] *See* Alan Greenblatt, *How State AGs Became a Check on the President*, GOVERNING (Sept. 30, 2021), https://www.governing.com/now/how-state-ags-became-a-check-on-the-president.

[121] Colin Binkley, *More Republican States Challenge New Title IX Rules Protecting LGBTQ+ Students*, AP NEWS (April 20, 2024), https://apnews.com/article/title-ix-lawsuit-transgender-sports-f47922529d12b68580a4fb5bc5981ba5.

are permitted to sue on behalf of themselves and other similarly in-jured persons[122]. These suits model themselves on an old English form of lawsuit known as relator or, in Latin, *qui tam* action. The ba-sic idea is simple: the government, which could sue to enforce a sov-ereign injury, delegates its enforcement power to a private individual who litigates the case in the government's shoes. If the individual (called a relator), wins, he receives a bounty in the form of a share of the damages ordered by the court. (It bears emphasis that back in 1978, during the Carter Administration, lawyers in the U.S. Depart-ment of Justice unsuccessfully sought to amend Rule 23 to authorize a public action modeled on the relator action; under this proposal the federal government would have had authority to screen the action and to take over the litigation or to dismiss it[123]).

As one example of this trend, in 2004 California authorized a state relator action as part of its labor law, enabling an aggrieved employee to file actions for civil penalties on behalf of themselves, other employees, and the State against employers for violations of the California labor code[124]. Known as the Private Attorney Gen-eral Act ("PAGA"), the statute navigates two obstacles that such a lawsuit might face in federal court. First, the Supreme Court has held that as a matter of constitutional standing, a federal plantiff may not seek to recover a statutory penalty for a violation of an act unless that party has suffered a separate, concrete injury—usually of a financial sort[125]. Second, the majority of employment contracts in

---

[122] *See* Myriam E. Gilles & Gary Friedman, *The New* Qui Tam: *A Model for the Enforcement of Group Rights in a Hostile Era*, 98 TEX. L. REV. 489, 492 (2020) (explaining how relator actions function under the False Claims Act).

[123] David Freeman Engstrom, *Jacobins at Justice: The (Failed) Class Action Revo-lution of 1978 and the Puzzle of American Procedural Political Economy*, 165 U. PA. L. REV. 1531 (2017) (describing these events).

[124] CAL. LAB. CODE §§ 2698-99 (West 2011); *see also* Gilles & Friedman, *supra* note 122, at 493-94.

[125] Spokeo, Inc. v. Robins, 578 U.S. 330, 341 (2016) (rejecting the premise "that a plaintiff automatically satisfies the injury-in-fact requirement [of Article

the United States include mandatory arbitration clauses that foreclose litigation of workplace disputes[126]. The theory of the PAGA action is that the state's sovereign interest has been violated, and the state is not a party to the mandatory arbitration clause of the employment contract—rather, as in a federal relator action, the state may assign its interest to a private party for statutory enforcement, subject to public oversight[127].

Cases illustrating this second trend require a showing of injury (even if not at the level required in federal court) and are subject to some public oversight; it is important to distinguish them from the third trend I identify—state mechanisms that deputize private enforcement without requiring the plaintiff to show personal injury and without providing public oversight. The Texas Heartbeat Act, referred to as "S.B. 8", illustrates this quite different mechanism[128]. Texas enacted S.B. 8 before the Supreme Court overturned the right to an abortion. The Texas statute bars physicians from providing abortions without performing a test to determine the presence of a fetal heartbeat or upon detection of a fetal heartbeat. Moreover, it creates a right of action on behalf of any private citizen who can sue anyone who performs an abortion or intends to aid and abet that process, and, if successful, the claimant will receive a bounty of "not less than $10,000" per violation proven, paid by the abortion provider or anyone assisting the provider. When Texas enacted S.B. 8, the state effectively delegated enforcement authority in an area in which the state had no legitimate authority or sovereign interest—the statute

---

III of the U.S. Constitution] whenever a statute grants a person a statutory right and purports to authorize that person to sue to vindicate that right").

[126] Alexander J.S. Colvin, Econ. Policy Inst., The Growing Use of Mandatory Arbitration 5 (2018), https://www.epi.org/files/pdf/144131.pdf.

[127] Luke Norris, *The Promise and Perils of Private Enforcement*, 108 Va. L. Rev. 1483, 1486 (2022) (detailing how the Act "lacks public enforcement mechanisms, in large part to stop pre-enforcement suits against government officials").

[128] *See* Gilles & Friedman, *supra* note 122, at 521-22 (explaining the "assignment theory" of *qui tam* actions).

sought to block access to abortions after six weeks of pregnancy, in violation of federal rights protected under the Fourteenth Amendment[129].

For present purposes, what is important is that both PAGA and S.B. 8 illustrate new forms of action that serve the purposes of aggregation in the sense of affecting large groups of individuals who may not formally be named in the action, and combine regulatory goals with deterrence and compensation. PAGA explicitly aggregates claims and reflects a public-private collaboration for enforcement. S.B. 8 imposes liability on physicians and others and authorizes private enforcement, using the form of a single-plaintiff action to deter the provision of medical services to multiple pregnant persons and so in practical effect achieves aggregated relief.

So much for aggregation in state courts or by state officials. I see another emergent aggregative trend in federal administrative agencies. As with state courts, the sheer number of claims resolved by administrative agencies underscores the importance of aggregation as a way to secure access and relief. Like state courts, administrative agencies decide more cases each year than the federal courts—in 2013, the Social Security Administration, one of more than 400 federal agencies, decided 800,00 cases, or twice the civil docket of all federal courts combined[130]. Some agencies have authority to bring enforcement actions directed at single companies or indi-

---

[129] *Id.*, at 1532 (arguing that in *qui tam* actions like those authorized under S.B. 8, "the enforcer has received no concrete harm to them apart from personal disgust or negative feelings . . . at having discovered that a person had an abortion . . . . In addition, in those contexts, enforcers are not vindicating a settled public interest--such as one in safe air and water or preventing fraud on the government. They are either enforcing unconstitutional laws or laws that are in the mix of larger public contest and may well be unconstitutional").

[130] *See* Richard H. Fallon, Jr., John Manning, Daniel Meltzer & David Shapiro, Hart and Wechsler's The Federal Courts and the Federal System 39 (7th ed. 2015).

viduals, although the Supreme Court has begun to chip away at this authority[131].

I want to draw attention to the less conventional agency action that seeks enforcement *en masse* and relies on aggregation. More than seventy agencies have adopted procedural rules authorizing consolidation, class actions, or aggregate mechanisms that require the showing of a common question of law or fact[132]. Admittedly as of 2018, not many agencies had actually put these procedures to use—although those that have, have done so to significant effect. The Equal Employment Opportunity Commission, for example, has deployed a class action procedure, modeled on Federal Rule 23, to challenge and resolve what are known as "pattern and practice" discrimination claims[133]. As with California PAGA actions, there are reasons to think that administrative aggregation could become more prominent this decade—the agency is not required to follow the Supreme Court's recent decisions narrowing the scope of standing or toughening the standards for class certification[134]. At the same time, the

---

[131] *See, e.g.*, AMG Capital Mgmt., LLC v. FTC, 593 U.S. 67 (2021) (holding that section 13(b) of the Federal Trade Commission Act did not authorize the FTC directly to obtain court-ordered monetary relief because the language referred only to injunctions); SEC v. Jarkesy, 144 S. Ct. 2117 (2024) (holding that the Seventh Amendment requires that the SEC bring civil antifraud suits against defendants in Article III courts, not administrative hearings).

[132] *See* Michael Sant'Ambrogio & Adam S. Zimmerman, *Inside the Agency Class Action*, 126 Yale L.J. 1634, 1659 (2017). One might analogize these procedures to the Judicial Panel on Multi-District Litigation's use of consolidation of actions that share common questions of law or fact. *See* 28 U.S.C. § 1407.

[133] *See* 29 C.F.R. § 1614.204 (2012). The EEOC adopted the rule in response to a lawsuit filed in the 1970s by the NAACP against the Civil Service Commission, challenging employment discrimination by NASA. *See* Adam Zimmerman, *Group Justice in Administrative Courts*, Amer. Const. Soc'y (Oct. 4, 2018), https://www.acslaw.org/expertforum/group-justice-in-administrative-courts/.

[134] A change in presidential administrations would likewise alter the enforcement landscape in significant ways. *See* Zachary Halaschak, *Trump and*

Court's recent decisions questioning the authority of administrative agencies could effectively block this (or any) administrative enforcement strategy.

I identify a third trend—one that takes us out of public courts and public agencies and into the domain of private decision making—namely alternative dispute resolution (ADR for short), especially arbitration. You are aware that the United States is exceptional relative to the European Union in accepting, and indeed encouraging, the inclusion of mandatory arbitration clauses in boilerplate consumer and employment contracts. These provisions govern any dispute that might arise between the parties, and bear none of the markers of traditional consent; the terms are adhesive and nonnegotiable[135]. The Supreme Court has been the driver of this trend through its reinterpretation of the Federal Arbitration Act (FAA)[136]. Critically, in 2011, the Court in *AT&T Mobility v. Concepcion* upheld arbitration clauses in standard form consumer contracts that ban consumers from litigating as a class[137].

GOP would seek to unravel administrative state after years of Biden-era rulemaking, WASH. EXAMINER (May 9, 2024), https://www.washingtonexaminer.com/policy/finance-and-economy/2996883/trump-gop-seek-unravel-administrative-state/#google_vignette. *See also* Helen Hershkoff & Luke Norris, *The Beleaguered Sovereign: Judicial Restraints on Public Enforcement*, 103 TEX. L. REV. – (2025, forthcoming) (arguing that a core legacy of the Roberts Court will be its "undermining marketplace regulation by making it increasingly difficult for individuals and administrative agencies to redress statutory violations and implement regulatory policy", while also making it difficult for government lawyers to bring enforcement actions) (manuscript on file with the author).

[135] For discussion of these developments, see Hershkoff & Norris, *supra* note 21; Helen Hershkoff & Judith Resnik, *Contractualisation of Civil Litigation in the United States: Procedure, Contract, Public Authority, Aggregate Litigation, and Power*, in CONTRACTUALISATION OF CIVIL LITIGATION 419 (Anna Nylund & Antonio Cabral eds., 2023).

[136] The Federal Arbitration Act currently is codified in Title 9 of the U.S. Code.

[137] AT&T Mobility LLC v. Concepcion, 563 U.S. 333 (2011).

Against this background, reconsider California's enactment of a private attorney general act and focus on whether a mandatory arbitration clause in an individual employment contract can ban a PAGA suit by a private individual as a form of group, representative, or aggregative action. That question has been the subject of litigation in both the California Supreme Court and the Supreme Court of the United States. In 2014, the California Supreme Court, in a case called *Iskanian v. CLS Transportation*[138], addressed a PAGA claim brought by a worker whose employment contract included a broad arbitration agreement that banned "representative actions". The California Supreme Court held that a PAGA claim lies outside the FAA's coverage because it is not a dispute between an employer and an employee arising out of their contractual relationship, but rather is a dispute between an employer and the state. Then, in 2022, in a case called *Viking River Cruises, Inc. v. Moriana*[139], the U.S. Supreme Court addressed the relation between the FAA and PAGA. The Court, eight-to-one, held that the FAA requires arbitration of an individual worker's contractual claim, but left it to the California courts to decide whether the individual workers could also bring a PAGA claim in court on a representative basis. The next year, in 2023, the California Supreme Court, in *Adolph v. Uber Technologies*[140], unanimously held that a worker retains statutory standing to bring a PAGA claim even when the individual's contractual claim is subject to mandatory arbitration. These decisions have created space for other states to enact California-style "relator" actions to redress violations of labor and employment laws, although none so far have followed California's lead.

Nevertheless, aggregation is affecting arbitral practice even where a consumer or workplace document purports to ban class actions. Recall that Professor Miller emphasized in his Keynote Address the

---

[138] 327 P.3d 129 (Cal. 2014).
[139] 596 U.S. 639 (2022).
[140] 532 P.3d 682 (Cal. 2023).

entrepreneurial nature of legal practice in the United States. That kind of professional creativity is at the core of the next trend that I identify. In particular, plaintiffs' counsel, foreclosed from filing class actions in federal court or class actions before an arbitral panel instead are filing single arbitration claims, but bundling them together as if a mass action. As described by one commentary, counsel are "filing hundreds or thousands of separate arbitration demands on behalf of similarly situated claimants alleging identical claims against companies"—in particular, under arbitration agreements that require the company to pay the bulk of the filing or neutrals' fees[141]. The practice of "mass" or "bundled" claims has produced some ironic results; companies that mandated arbitration but now must pay large and unexpected filing fees are disavowing their agreements in favor of federal litigation. The situation is dynamic, and as with class action practice generally, defendant groups have sought structural change to blunt the success of the group mechanism. In particular, companies have sought to amend the terms of their contracts and even the governing arbitration rules either to ban the filing of bundled arbitration claims or to withhold the payment of fees; moreover, they are insisting on using bellwether hearings[142].

So far, I have surveyed new forms of aggregation in state courts, federal agencies, and arbitration. All of these devices involve large numbers of similarly affected plaintiffs. The fourth and final mechanism I will discuss does not share that important characteristic. Here the big news is the so-called nationwide injunction, in some quarters called the universal injunction, entered by a single federal district

---

[141] *See* Zachary D. Miller, Kevin S. Ranlett & Rachel R. Friedman, *Mass Arbitration: Altering the Litigation Landscape*, 78 BUS. LAW. 515 (2023) (surveying mass arbitration cases).

[142] *See, e.g.*, Cheryl Wilson, *Mass Arbitration: How the Newest Frontier of Mandatory Arbitration Jurisprudence Has Created a Brand New Private Enforcement Regime in the Gig Economy Era*, 69 UCLA L. REV. 372 (2022) (discussing the mass arbitration strategy from both parties' perspective).

court at the behest of a single plaintiff[143]. Use of this remedy is most prominent in lawsuits challenging policies and practices of the federal government. By practical effect, a single district judge can block the United States from enforcing federal law—whether in a statute or regulation—not just with respect to the plaintiff in a single district, but across the country, and for the most part, these actions have bypassed the procedural protections of Federal Rule 23[144]. The current surge in lawsuits seeking nationwide injunctions reflects the hyperpolarized state of U.S. politics and judicial decisionmaking: according to a study published in the Harvard Law Review, such orders "are overwhelmingly issued by judges appointed by a President from the opposite political party as the President who promulgated the policy at issue"[145]. Use of a nationwide injunction to revise law on a broad scale without due process protections or electoral oversight raises significant questions about fairness, access, and democratic commitments. This is not to deny that the nationwide injunction could have a legitimate role in securing relief *en masse*[146]—but, as with all procedural mechanisms, details of practice are not merely

---

[143] For a definition, see Joanna R. Lampe, Cong. Rsch. Serv., LSB10664, *Nationwide Injunction: Recent Legal Developments* (Dec. 2, 2021), https://crsreports.con gress.gov/product/pdf/LSB/LSB10664.

[144] *District Court Reform: Nationwide Injunctions*, 137 HARV. L. REV 1701, 1709 n. 2 (2024) (identifying a few cases in which plaintiffs certified a nationwide class before obtaining the nationwide injunction).

[145] *Id.* at 1707; *see also* Charlton C. Copeland, *Seeing Beyond Courts: The Political Context of the Nationwide Injunction*, 91 U. COLO. L. REV. 789 (2020) (discussing the dual problems of "unilateral presidential authority" and "increased partisan, polarization in Congress").

[146] For scholarly defenses of the nationwide injunction as a way to redress irreparable harm and provide relief, see, for example, Amanda Frost, *In Defense of Nationwide Injunctions*, 93 N.Y.U. L. REV. 1065, 1098-101 (2018); Suzette M. Malveaux, *Class Actions, Civil Rights, and the National Injunction*, 131 HARV. L. REV. F. 56 (2017); Spencer E. Amdur & David Hausman, *Nationwide Injunctions and Nationwide Harm*, 131 HARV. L. REV. F. 49 (2017); Zayn Siddique, *Nationwide Injunctions*, 117 COLUM. L. REV. 2095 (2017).

technical concerns but rather issues that implicate profound substantive values[147].

When I entered the class action scene forty years ago, the structural reform suit remained a vital mechanism for protecting and enforcing rights, although the Supreme Court had begun to circumscribe its use in significant ways. Despite those doctrinal cutbacks, injunctive class actions challenging unconstitutional or illegal government practices persist and even occasionally win[148]. In 2011, for example, in a case called *Brown v. Plata*, the Supreme Court held that a court-mandated population limit was necessary to remedy a violation of prisoners' Eighth Amendment rights. Keep in mind, that the decision came as a surprise—the Supreme Court had not affirmed a lower court prison crowding order since 1978, and the decision eked by with a bare majority of the justices[149]. Yet even as the Supreme Court has made it more difficult to use the "(b)(2)" class as a mechanism for accountability and change, new approaches and practices are developing to fill the remedial gap—although in some cases they seem designed or are being applied to undermine, rather than protect, civil rights and civil liberties, and so are normatively problematic. Whether these new forms of aggregation will succeed and what the metric of success ought to be remain open questions. The situation is dynamic; at the least it highlights what Mauro Cappelletti and Bryant Garth emphasized in their now canonical discussions of collective action and access to justice—the

---

[147] *See* Helen Hershkoff, Luke Norris & Judith Resnik, *Procedure, Inequality, and Access*, L. & POL. ECON. BLOG (July 16, 2024), https://lpeproject.org/blog/procedure-inequality-and-access/ (explaining that procedure can effectuate or undermine fairness and due process values).

[148] *See* David Marcus, *Groups and Rights in Institutional Reform Litigation*, 97 NOTRE DAME L. REV. 619 (2022).

[149] Brown v. Plata, 563 U.S. 493 (2011); *see* Margo Schlanger, *Plata v. Brown and Realignment: Jails, Prisons, Courts, and Politics*, 48 HARV. C.R.-C.L. REV. 48, 165 (2013).

question is "how, at what price, and for whose benefit" the procedural system really works[150].

I began this Response making clear that I would offer neither praise nor criticism of Professor Miller and his Keynote Address. He is, of course, a beloved and esteemed colleague and he has been a powerful voice in seeking to ensure judicial access[151]. Yet let me say this: scholars have directed a great deal of criticism at Federal Rule 23. Those criticisms should not obscure the importance of the class action, together with organizing, public education, and legislation, in securing accountability, promoting fairness, and protecting rights. Without the class action, my clients at the Willowbrook State School might have remained institutionalized in inhumane conditions. For that and more, we should have only praise for Professor Miller and the mechanism of justice he helped to create.

Thank you for this opportunity to speak with you today.

---

[150] Mauro Cappelletti & Bryant Garth, *Access to Justice: The Newest Wave in the Worldwide Movement to Make Rights Effective*, 27 BUFF. L. REV. 181, 181 (1978).

[151] *See* Mary Kay Kane, *Foreword*, 90 OR. L. REV. 913, 913 (2012) (stating that Professor Miller has dedicated "his entire career … to trying to preserve and increase public access to justice").

www.ingramcontent.com/pod-product-compliance
Lightning Source LLC
Chambersburg PA
CBHW082326040426
42445CB00026B/1836